THE LONG RANGE
DESERT GROUP
IN NORTH AFRICA

THE LONG RANGE DESERT GROUP IN NORTH AFRICA

BRENDAN O'CARROLL

Pen & Sword
MILITARY

First published in Great Britain in 2023
and republished in this format in 2025 by
PEN & SWORD MILITARY
An imprint of
Pen & Sword Books Ltd
Yorkshire – Philadelphia

Copyright © Brendan O'Carroll, 2023

ISBN 978-1-39903-092-2

The right of Brendan O'Carroll to be identified as author of this work has been asserted by him in accordance with the Copyright, Designs and Patents Act 1988.

A CIP catalogue record for this book is available from the British Library.

All rights reserved. No part of this book may be reproduced, transmitted, downloaded, decompiled or reverse engineered in any form or by any means, electronic or mechanical including photocopying, recording or by any information storage and retrieval system, without permission from the Publisher in writing. No part of this book may be used or reproduced in any manner for the purpose of training artificial intelligence technologies or systems.

Typeset by Concept, Huddersfield, West Yorkshire, HD4 5JL
Printed and bound in England by CPI Group (UK) Ltd, Croydon CR0 4YY

The Publisher's authorised representative in the EU for product safety is Authorised Rep Compliance Ltd., Ground Floor, 71 Lower Baggot Street, Dublin D02 P593, Ireland.
www.arccompliance.com

For a complete list of Pen & Sword titles please contact
PEN & SWORD BOOKS LIMITED
47 Church Street, Barnsley, South Yorkshire, S70 2AS, England
E-mail: enquiries@pen-and-sword.co.uk
Website: www.pen-and-sword.co.uk
or
PEN AND SWORD BOOKS
1950 Lawrence Rd, Havertown, PA 19083, USA
E-mail: Uspen-and-sword@casematepublishers.com
Website: www.penandswordbooks.com

Contents

Acknowledgements vii
Introduction ix
1. The Long Range Patrol 1
2. Dress and Insignia 23
3. The Vehicles 39
4. The Heavy Section 81
5. Navigation 91
6. Signals 111
7. Supplies 125
8. Weapons 141
9. At Rest 159
10. The Road Watch 183
11. Enemy Encounters 197
12. The Libyan Taxi Service 221
Bibliography 243
Index 244

Acknowledgements

To my wife Margaret for undertaking the onerous job of proofreading; a big task that she carried out with great skill and patience. Also my children Diana, Michelle and Patrick for their continued support with my projects.

Thanks to Nick Hofmann for his technical skills in restoring the quality of some of the original photos, a number of which were in poor condition. Most of these were taken by LRDG men with their personal cameras, so many of the images are not of the same quality as those taken by official photographers.

I wish to thank Jonathan Pittaway of South Africa, the author of two books on the LRDG: *LRDG Rhodesia* (2002) and *Long Range Desert Group, Rhodesia: The Men Speak* (2009). He has kindly shared the S Patrol images published in this book and has been very helpful with my publications over the years.

Also thanks to Ian Chard from England, LRDG researcher and Y Patrol historian. He has been a very supportive contributor, providing copies of LRDG photos and other related research documents from British LRDG veterans. The Y Patrol images, via Ian, came from the wartime albums of Mick Allen, Harry Chard, Tich Cave, Brian and Marjorie Springford, Dick Lawson and Eric Wilson.

To Fiona Ashenden and her daughter Liana Ashenden for kindly sharing the extensive wartime LRDG photo collection and the personal accounts of their father and grandfather, Ron Davies of T2 Patrol.

A special thanks to the late LRDG veterans and their families for permission to publish their personal wartime photos and diaries. Norman Boyd and Andrew Boyd, Dave Burnnand and Wayne Burnnand, Merlyn Craw and Jack and Melody Craw, Leighton Burne, Mary and Ron Campbell, Walter Ellingham, Roger Evans, Merle Fogden, Myles and Maxine Gedye, Claude 'Bluey' Grimsey, Frank and Irene Jopling, Jann Keightley, Richard Lawson, Dick Lewis, Filani Macassey and Pat Macassey, Paddy Mackay and Dave Mackay, Ian McCulloch, Gordon Parkes, Tom Ritchie, Alf Saunders and Max Saunders, Don Steele and Roger Steele, Keith Tippett, Clarke Waetford and Charlie Waetford, Nick Wilder and Warner and Andrew Wilder, and Keith Yealands.

I also wish to acknowledge others for their contribution in supplying photos, information and sources that helped to make this work possible: Bob Amos-Jones, Charles Bird, Roberto Chiarvetto, Phil Deed, Paul Farmer, Kuno Gross, David Harrison, Mike Hughes, Glen Hunter, Phillip James, Peter Kirk, Mike Leet, Antonio Maraziti, Dave McCann, Ethan and Margot O'Carroll, Geoff Oldham, Jonathan Pittaway, Isabelle Subritzky, Emily Subritzky and the late Jack Valenti of the LRDG Preservation Society.

Introduction

The purpose of this book is to tell the story through images and explanatory captions of how the Long Range Desert Group operated in North Africa in the Second World War. They were initially a long-range reconnaissance and intelligence-gathering unit founded in July 1940. Then progressively, up to the end of the desert war in May 1943, they developed into a very formidable force in relation to its size and successfully completed multiple missions while operating deep behind enemy lines.

Their 'trips' took them away from base for weeks on end, which meant they had to be fully self-contained with equipment and supplies. They were experts in navigation, mapping, signals, desert concealment, survival, hit-and-run warfare against forts, road convoys and raiding enemy positions including airfields. In this book, the men's everyday life is portrayed in detail including meals, camping, dropping off agents, rescuing downed airmen, treating the wounded and getting stuck in the sand. This will give the reader a view into the tough yet rewarding life of an LRDG patrolman operating in one of the most harsh terrains and climates in the world.

To enable this, their independent patrols had to be fully equipped with the necessary stores, fuel, water, weapons, munitions and equipment, and their men highly trained and capable. Throughout the illustrated chapters, this work will tell the story of what they required to achieve their missions. It will also include details of how they dressed for the extremes of heat and cold and of the distinctive insignia they displayed. Furthermore, the vehicles they drove are described, along with the type of weapons they used and how they navigated in a harsh environment with few landmarks. Signalling was also of great importance in relaying their vital intelligence gained back to base.

Chapters include reference to the enemy they encountered and how they transported many other parties on secret missions or as observers and recovered downed airmen, an activity they referred to as the 'Libyan Taxi Service'.

The images are supported by comprehensive descriptive chapter introductions, including a number of transcriptions of original LRDG operational reports. These describe the actions in the words of the men themselves, as they were officially recorded at the time. This imparts a human face to the narrative, along with the words and illustrations that bring the story alive. For example, veteran Ron Davies of T2 Patrol recalled his overview of his time in the LRDG:

> The LRDG was a specialised group and it was considered an honour to get in. It was really good too, as we had the best food and supplies. It was a very

open unit where you were allowed to ask questions and know exactly what was going on. You were expected to take an intelligent interest in what was happening around you. For me, having served in Greece and Crete, I found being part of the LRDG was the most enjoyable part of the war.

A good number of the photos used have come from the private cameras of the LRDG men themselves, therefore the quality is usually not as good as those images taken by official army photographers or war correspondents. Nonetheless, the personal photos give a good reflection of the daily life and action of the LRDG in the field. Many of these are previously unpublished as they came from the photo albums of LRDG veterans. Others have been seen before in my earlier works or in other publications.

Brendan O'Carroll
2022

Chapter One

The Long Range Patrol

The Long Range Desert Group had its beginnings in July 1940, when Major Ralph Bagnold conceived the unit. He was a British army signals officer, geographer and desert explorer. Following the Italian entry into the war in June 1940, Egypt was now considered under threat as Libya had been an Italian colony since the 1920s. Consequently, the British Middle East GHQ needed urgent intelligence as to the enemy activity in southern Libya close to the Egyptian border.

Bagnold, along with a small group of fellow explorers, had ventured into Libya in the 1920s and 1930s, where they acquired considerable knowledge of desert travel, navigation and survival techniques. Armed with these abilities, he offered his services to General Sir Archibald Wavell, Commander-in-Chief Middle East, to lead a patrol far behind the lines to try to establish the Italian dispositions and intentions. With southern Libya well beyond the range of aerial observation, he immediately authorized Bagnold's plans for an overland reconnaissance unit to be formed, with six weeks to recruit and prepare the force. This became officially entitled the No. 1 Long Range Patrol Unit, also known as the LRP.

Its first volunteers answered a call which specified men 'who do not mind a hard life, scanty food, little water, lots of discomfort, and possess stamina and initiative.' Consequently, for the first six months of its operations the LRP was manned almost entirely by specially selected members from the Second New Zealand Expeditionary Force (2NZEF). These men had been training in Egypt since their arrival in early 1940 and were available for attachment. Because the initial long-range reconnaissance patrols had proved their worth, it was decided to continue and expand the force.

Major Bagnold was the commanding officer overseeing three patrols. The two fighting patrols were T and W, commanded by the prewar desert explorer Captain P.A. Clayton and by Captain E.C. Mitford (1st Royal Tank Regiment) respectively. There was also R Patrol, which was intended to carry supplies and was led by a New Zealander, Second Lieutenant D.G. Steele. The 'Kiwis' were not expected to command fighting patrols until they gained more experience in the desert. The adjutant and quartermaster was Lieutenant L.B. Ballantyne and the medical officer was Lieutenant F.B. Edmundson, both New Zealanders. The intelligence officer was Lieutenant W.B. Kennedy Shaw, who joined from the Colonial Service in Palestine.

The three LRP patrol vehicles bore Maori names beginning with the letters W, T and R. The trucks were also numbered; for example, W Patrol displayed a white letter and number in a black painted rectangle, 'W2'. T Patrol showed in a black diamond and R Patrol in a black circle. These were painted on either side of the bonnet. This insignia style was discontinued with the introduction of the Ford trucks in early 1941. The first patrols consisted of twenty-seven to thirty-two men travelling in eleven desert-adapted Chevrolet WA trucks. They were led by a commander's pilot vehicle, a Ford 01 V8 15cwt. Furthermore, each patrol included a wireless truck and a fitter's truck that carried tools and spare parts to enable repairs to be done beyond the range of assistance.

A headquarters' unit oversaw the patrols. In addition, there was a Heavy Section (logistical support trucks) under Lieutenant C.A. Holliman. These were employed to transport supplies to bases and to establish forward hidden dumps, which helped to extend the range of operations to great distances.

Ground reconnaissance was the principal objective of the force: to provide, by way of patrols, detailed charting and information about enemy dispositions from deep behind the lines in the Libyan Desert. This small but extremely effective unit of British and Empire troops was to run reconnaissance and survey patrols with great regularity from Cairo to Tripoli over some of the most challenging and arid landscape in the world. Each patrol was a completely self-contained independent body capable of travelling hundreds of kilometres deep into enemy territory over all types of difficult desert terrain. They were experts in navigation, desert survival and warfare. This was only possible due to their well-maintained and desert-modified trucks. These vehicles were skilfully driven and navigated by tough, self-reliant men who adapted well to desert life with its extreme climatic and geographical conditions.

Apart from reconnaissance trips and setting up forward dumps, the LRP's first direct action role was to place mines on the roads used by Italian convoys or to lay ambush against them. In September, W Patrol came across a landing ground about halfway between Tazerbo and Kufra. There they encountered two 6-ton lorries belonging to a civilian firm, the Trucchi Company, which ran a fortnightly supply convoy to Kufra. A burst of machine-gun fire resulted in the capture of two Italians and five Arabs, a goat, 2,500 gallons of petrol and other stores. However, more importantly, they found the official mail from Kufra and Uweinat which gave details of Italian dispositions in the inner desert. The trucks were hidden and the seven prisoners were taken back to Cairo.

Towards the end of October, R and T Patrols made simultaneous sorties in southern and northern Libya. While undertaking such an operation on 31 October 1940, Captain D.G. Steele's R Patrol found an enemy bomb dump buried in the sand. They dug up seventy-five 18kg bombs and 640 2kg bombs along with ten 44-gallon drums of petrol, all of which were destroyed. Later that same day they burned an unguarded Savoia-Marchetti SM.79 bomber and 160 drums of fuel. Gunner C.O. 'Bluey' Grimsey was with R Patrol during this discovery and its aftermath. He recorded the events in his diary:

> On Thursday, after a hurried breakfast of porridge and curried fish, we set out at 0630 hrs on our patrolling duties, looking for fresh tracks and suitable

places to lay our mines. We had little real success until just before noon whilst coasting along in 'air' formation, when our skipper in front gave the halt signal and we all stopped. Still in scattered formation, we watched him dismount and proceed to investigate two innocent-looking petrol drums and then start to dig round in the sand with his hands. We, in our Bofors gun truck, were immediately behind Captain Steele, and soon saw him run back to his truck for his shovel which he used to excavate a box from beneath the slight mound near the drums, then another and another. Opening one, we found it neatly packed with bombs wrapped like eggs, their detonators and firing mechanisms similarly packed in separate compartments. Soon the squad had unearthed a whole dump of aerial bombs of various calibres, along with 44 gallons of aero petrol.

While a few trucks kept a lookout from a distance, the cases of bombs were all excavated and placed atop of the petrol, with detonators exposed in such a position that they could be made a target for the Vickers guns. One was mounted on the skipper's Ford, the idea being to ignite and blow up the dump with tracer fire from a safe distance. We retreated some 800 yards. Captain Steele sent a burst of fire towards the exposed boxes. Woomph! Flame belched 400ft skyward, followed by dense black smoke. We turned tail and made for the hills. Some of the bombs which were falling all around, filled with TNT, might explode too near to be healthy, so we took no chances. As we sped to the rocks, I watched the black smoke curling 1,000ft into the still hot air. There was another explosion and a colossal mushroom of flame seethed skyward, sending out rockets of flame.

After lunch we again struck south towards where we knew there should be a landing ground. Away in the distance could be seen dancing mirages so common at that time of day in the flat country. Huge lakes appeared and floating islands apparently suspended by invisible sky hooks gradually came down to connect with the earth as we approached. Then there was another strange mirage, not unlike a spout of water reflecting the rays of the sun. We all gazed at this and wondered what our skipper proposed to do. As we approached, it slowly took shape as some shiny object reflecting the sun. Soon we could see it was some type of aircraft on the ground. We stopped within 1,000 yards and Captain Steele sent a burst from the Vickers gun in the direction of the plane. There was no movement or sign of life, so we cautiously advanced. We had come across a Savoia [Savoia-Marchetti SM.79] Italian plane of the heavy bomber type, quite modern, but with a damaged undercarriage and probably awaiting repairs. Those responsible were little dreaming that enemy troops would make it necessary for them to put a guard on the machine so many hundreds of miles from enemy territory.

We fired Verey lights into the petrol tanks and the plane became a hot, molten mess. After searching the landing ground, we found four 44-gallon drums of aero petrol which we promptly fired by sending tracer shells into them. In less than an hour we had rendered useless about £15,000 worth of enemy material. Altogether that day we reckoned we had inflicted £30,000 worth of damage to the enemy. Although it was reported shots had been fired from the hills while we were destroying the landing ground, there were no casualties.

That evening we carefully laid some of our land mines along the transport routes, the tracks of which we could plainly see in the sand. Having refilled some tins of water we found in the Italian landing ground, we set course north-west and camped for the night some 80 kilometres from the scene of operations.

On Friday 1 November while having a break after crossing some rough country, someone yelled 'Look, there's a plane!' Like lightning, we ran to our vehicles and made for the low hills covered with loose rocks which we considered would give us some protection. We got there without a hitch and no sooner had we done so than three enemy planes appeared: two heavy machines and a smaller one of the Ghibli type.

At first they circled overhead at 1,000 to 1,500ft and some of us thought we were so well concealed by our natural camouflage of the rock, but such was evidently not the case as for the second time they circled and descended to 1,000ft. The first big plane let loose a stick of bombs which fell all around the trucks without hitting one. Captain Steele fired a burst from his Vickers gun which immediately had the desired result of making the plane climb higher. Perceiving that they intended to bomb us at a fairly high altitude and having regard for our natural camouflage, our only hope was to lie quite still away from our trucks and wait for the worst, knowing that a movement would only reveal our positions and realising that our fire would have little effect at such range. Four times they circled, each plane dropping many small anti-personnel bombs while we lay flat, still availing ourselves of such cover as the rocks would allow.

Little bits of rock and splinters came ricocheting and whining all around us and for the best part of an hour we lay there helpless as the minutes dragged by. Then another plane passed, unloading its deathly hail and another's engines grew louder as it approached to attack. At last they circled for the last time, still keeping high and headed back towards Uweinat. One by one, we came out from behind our rocks and breathed a sigh of relief when we realised no one had been hit. By a miracle our trucks also were intact, although I am sure the enemy must have thought they had destroyed them, with such a shower of dust and smoke that the bombs had put up all around them. Apart from puncturing a few of our water tins and embedding pieces of shrapnel in our tyres, we were able to proceed, which we did at a hot pace.

In the meantime, Captain P.A. Clayton's T Patrol had laid mines on the Jalo-Ajedabia road and distributed pamphlets written in Arabic inciting the tribes to make trouble in Libya. On 1 November 1940, the column attacked a small Italian fort at Augila, where after the first burst of machine-gun fire and rounds from the truck-mounted 37mm Bofors gun, the astonished garrison ran off to a nearby native village. Clayton captured two Schwarzlose machine guns, rifles, a revolver and stores, along with one Libyan soldier for interrogation.

Between 28 October and 4 November 1940, the LRP worked with the RAF to undertake mapping and reconnoitre for possible landing grounds. An obsolete Vickers Valentia from No. 216 (Bomber Transport) Squadron RAF was employed to carry out this work. The aircraft was fitted with long-range tanks and was refuelled from three dumps previously laid by the LRP for that specific purpose. It had a crew of six who worked in liaison with Captain E.C. Mitford and the medical officer Captain F.B. Edmundson. Because of load concerns it was impossible to carry enough water for the whole operation, so it was supplied by the ground patrols when they made contact with the aircraft.

With the aid of the Valentia, more topographical information was obtained about the recently found Kalansho Sand Sea. In other areas, the 'going' was plotted for future mapping and further landing grounds were located. The aircraft flew eight missions that covered a distance of 3,070 kilometres, with a total flying time of twenty-five hours. They were lucky not to encounter enemy aircraft who would have made short work of such a slow lumbering target.

In late November, led by Captain E.C. Mitford, W Patrol visited Uweinat where for more than an hour they were attacked by three enemy aircraft. Though many small bombs were dropped, skilful, evasive driving resulted in no damage being done. The patrol then went on to the Italian outpost at Ain Dua, which at first appeared deserted. A round from the 37mm Bofors gun was fired, which brought an immediate response of enemy rifle and machine-gun fire. The garrison, estimated to be thirty men with three machine guns, was well-established in positions among large boulders, stone walls and trenches. Consequently, a frontal attack over an open plain was not an option.

Lieutenant J.H. Sutherland commanded D Troop consisting of three trucks and eight men. They moved against the enemy's left flank, while the rest of the patrol gave covering fire. The troop worked its way through the rocks on foot. Yet despite coming under steady fire, they managed to drive the Italians up the hill into fresh positions, leaving three casualties including one dead.

Two Italian bombers and then later a reconnaissance plane appeared overhead, so the patrol quickly withdrew and hid among the rocks. After several hours the sky was clear again and a second attack on Ain Dua was launched. The plan was to attack from both flanks while still covered from the centre. With its Bofors gun in support, D Troop attacked over the ground where it had been before. While one truck and a Bofors gun gave covering fire from the plain, the rest of the patrol worked their way around the right flank. Sutherland reached the edge of the fortifications and inflicted casualties from grenades launched from an EY grenade-launching rifle, but he was then pinned down by return fire.

Trooper L.A. Willcox crawled with his .303 Lewis gun to within 18 metres of an enemy machine-gun emplacement, then stood up, fired his weapon from the hip

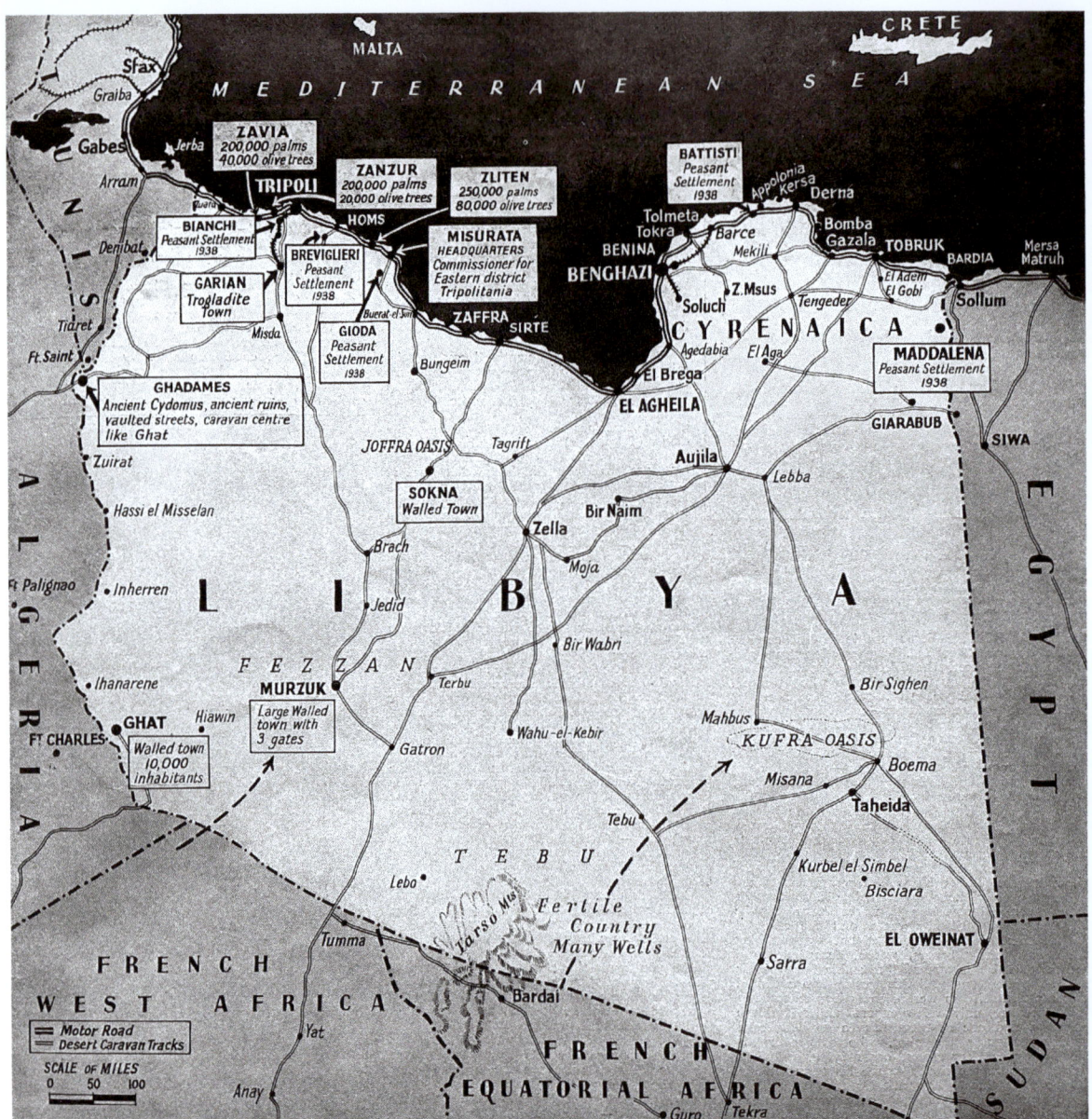

Wartime map of Libya, as published in the British *The Sphere* magazine on 1 March 1941.

and killed the crew of four. Sutherland moved in closer, but he was again cut off by enemy fire. Willcox came to his rescue a second time by silencing a further machine-gun position.

Owing to the almost impassable massive rocks, the remainder of the patrol was unable to get close enough to engage the Italians. The garrison was well-placed and defended themselves so capably that it was impossible to take the position without incurring heavy losses. Accordingly, at dusk, W Patrol withdrew, leaving six of the enemy killed and at least six wounded without taking any casualties themselves. As a result of this action, Sutherland received the first Military Cross and Willcox the first Military Medal awarded to the LRP/LRDG.

The new formation – now to be known as the Long Range Desert Group – was established in November 1940. In December, under the command of Captain M.D.D. Crichton-Stuart, recruits from the Coldstream and Scots Guards regiments joined the unit, expanding the force as G (Guards) Patrol. They took over the vehicles and equipment of W Patrol which was disbanded. Its members either returned to their parent units or reinforced R or T Patrol. On 31 January 1941, a second new patrol was formed known as the S (South Rhodesian) Patrol under the command of Captain C.A. Holliman. The third new patrol, Y (Yeomanry), was introduced on 25 February 1941 under the command of Captain P.J.D. McCraith. They became one of the first Special Forces of the Second World War.

By the end of October 1941, the LRDG strength had peaked at about 350 personnel and patrol sizes were now split into ten half-patrols, with each having fifteen to eighteen men in five vehicles. The designations were changed to G1, G2, R1, R2, S1, S2, T1, T2, Y1 and Y2. The New Zealand patrols comprised A Squadron, while the Guards, Yeomanry and Rhodesians became B Squadron. Each patrol incorporated specialists, a navigator, radio-operator, medical orderly and a vehicle mechanic (fitter), each of whom manned a truck equipped for their role, plus a command or pilot vehicle. An expanded Group HQ oversaw the patrols and was supported by a Signals Troop, Light Repair Squadron and an Air Section of two Waco liaison aircraft. In addition, there was a Heavy Section that transported supplies to forward hidden dumps and between bases.

W Patrol members. Left: navigator Trooper J.W. Eyles and second-in-command Lieutenant J.H. Sutherland. The man displaying the NZ silver fern on his jersey is unidentified. On the truck left: gunner Trooper G.C. Garvin and driver Trooper A.F. Dodunski.

(**Opposite, above**) W Patrol Ford 01 V8 15cwt command car. Patrol commander Captain E.C. Mitford stands alongside. Note the coiled sand mats and the patrol flag.

(**Opposite, below**) Sergeant A.D. 'Buster' Gibb stands on his Chevrolet WA truck with W3 marked in a black rectangle. He rests his hand by the strapped .303 Lewis gun.

(**Above**) Left: W Patrol fitter Trooper L.F. Mather and gunner Trooper L.A. Willcox. They stand in front of their Chevrolet WA truck with the headlights covered to prevent reflection. Willcox won the first Military Medal in the LRDG for his role in the action at Ain Dua in November 1940.

Left: Lance Corporal C.H. Croucher and Lieutenant J.H. 'Sahara' Sutherland. Trooper A.M. Saunders stands in the back of the truck. Note the Shell fuel boxes on the side. Croucher was an ex-Merchant Marine and the chief navigator who trained the other LRP navigators. He rose through the ranks and by the end of the war he was the LRDG Adjutant and Intelligence Officer.

Navigator Lance Corporal C.H. Croucher, driver Trooper A.M. Saunders and wireless-operator Corporal F.R. Beech. Note the Italian number plate souvenir on the grill. Also unusual to see the canvas hood erected on the truck. Beech was later killed in action at Jebel Sherif on 31 January 1941.

Lieutenant J.H. Sutherland and driver Trooper C. Waetford. Note the captured Italian Campo sign decorating the truck. Sutherland won the first Military Cross in the LRDG for the action at Ain Dua in November 1940. Waetford was responsible for the naming of NZ trucks with Maori names and later won the Military Medal in an LRDG action.

W Patrol, 1940. Back row, from left: unknown, Trooper L.F. Mather, Gunner G.H. Nelson, Corporal A.D. Gibb, Sergeant A. McCorkindale, Private F.R. Brown, Bombardier A.E. Respinger, Captain E.G. Mitford, Trooper G.C. Garven, Trooper A.M. Saunders, Corporal F.R. Beech, Gunner J.W. Eyles. Middle row: Trooper V.C. Spain, Private J. Emslie, Lance Corporal E.G. Butler, Gunner C.O. Grimsey, Trooper A.F. Dodunski, Trooper C. Waetford. Front row: Trooper G.M. Barnes, Trooper R.O. Gorringe, Lance Corporal L. Roderick, Trooper G.C. Parkes, Trooper L.A. Willcox, Lieutenant J.H. Sutherland.

Major D.G. Steele. He led R Patrol with the formation of the Long Range Patrol in July 1940. Promoted in August 1941, he became Commanding Officer A (NZ) Squadron, LRDG. He was awarded the OBE in recognition of his services while in command at Siwa and later in Jalo.

Two Italian civilian Trucchi Company Fiat 634N trucks captured by W Patrol. These were painted red.

R Patrol Captain D.G. Steele (left) examines a dug-up concealed Italian bomb and fuel dump.

R Patrol members show off aircraft bombs uncovered in a buried dump. The munitions were later destroyed.

R Patrol Chevrolet WA displaying R4 in a circle, *Rotowai*. Private A.F. Brown sits on the spare wheel.

Captain D.G. Steele camped for the night against his Ford 01 V8 command car.

T Patrol members lean against an R Patrol truck R4 *Rotowai*. Left: Trooper J.L.P. Maccassey, Gunner E.C. Stutterd and Private L.J. Hawkins.

(**Above**) A .37mm Bofors gun truck joins up with the patrol.

(**Opposite, above**) R Patrol members: Captain D.G. Steele and Captain F.B. Edmundson, the medical officer, sit third and fourth from the right.

(**Opposite, below**) An aircraft visual sign created from flimsy cans. Trooper C. Waetford walks in front.

R Patrol column halted after a 13-kilometre climb in low gear up the escarpment from the Kharga Oasis. Note the crying skull art on the back of the truck.

T Patrol column of Chevrolet WA trucks with the Ford 01 V8 command car in front. The large guns are .55 Boys anti-tank rifles.

LRP patrol stuck in soft sand. The sand channels and mats are placed to negotiate a way out.

An Italian prisoner stands alongside a T Patrol Ford V8 command car.

Lieutenant R.B. McQueen, T Patrol, holding a sword captured from the Italian fort at Augila, along with the Schwarzlose machine gun on the left.

Desert vista as the patrol forms up.

The desert could be a harsh and fatal environment if unprepared. An LRP photo of a skeleton found half-buried in the sand.

Chapter Two

Dress and Insignia

The men who joined the LRDG wore the regular British army uniform of their parent units. However, specifically for this unit they were issued leather open-toed sandals called chapplies, which were more suitable than army boots for movement in the hot soft sand. In 1941 the mustard-coloured Arab head-dress (*keffiyeh*) was introduced. It was held in place by a black rope like agal. This was worn as parade dress and at other times as a matter of personal choice. It was useful when on patrol as it gave protection from the sun, dust, sand and flies and was also good in cold weather. However, in warmer conditions they could get stuffy or become entangled when working with engines or heavy weapons. Prior to this the LRDG wore a variety of headdress, including the standard army-issue caps/sidecaps, 'caps, comforter', beret or the topee pith helmet. For the New Zealanders, the 'Lemon Squeezer' army-issue felt hat was common wear. It was also not unusual for troopers to adopt, with the insignia removed, Italian or Afrika Korps caps as casual wear. By 1943, the *keffiyeh* was replaced by the black RTR (Royal Tank Regiment) pattern beret as the official headdress, though it was still used in the field if preferred. In addition, to protect the men when driving in the desert dust or in the glare of the sun, goggles and sunglasses were also on issue. In January 1942 a stores report listed, among other things, 100 pairs of 'tinted spectacles' for issue to S and T Patrols.

In colder weather a mix of clothing was worn including battledress, jerseys, leather jerkins, overalls, greatcoats and balaclavas. As an alternative to the army-issue greatcoats, a British 'Tropal' sheepskin-lined coat or a locally-acquired 'Hebron' sheep or goatskin coat was also supplied. During the winter they could remain dressed in these, both day and night. Sometimes the men looked more like polar explorers than desert adventurers. In the summer, as the day warmed up, the layers were peeled off and by midday they would be down to only shorts and sandals. 'Dress Regulations' did not exist when the LRDG was on patrol. Comfort was the main consideration. Water rationing prevented shaving, so this, together with their state of dress, often made the men look like a band of wandering vagrants. This could be an advantage, especially when spotted from the air as the enemy might see them as troops with no distinctive uniform and which could be their own, driving captured Allied vehicles.

Upon its formation in July 1940, there was no LRDG insignia. Any badges that were worn usually reflected the men's parent unit. The first badge was a commemorative or 'sweetheart' badge to mark the existence of the Long Range Patrol. It was unofficial and made for those who served with W, R and T Patrols, plus LRP HQ. When the Guards Patrol joined in November 1940, the unit became known as the LRDG. The LRP badge was designed in September 1940 by Gunner C.O. 'Bluey' Grimsey with the help of Dr F.B. Edmundson, the LRP medical officer. At first the badge was rejected by Colonel Bagnold for security reasons. However, he later gave approval because it was unofficial and was only to serve as a keepsake for family and sweethearts but was not to be worn on the uniform.

Claude 'Bluey' Grimsey wrote on 16 June 1949 his recollections regarding the creation of the LRP/LRDG badge:

> I was the original designer of the LRDG badge and its history is worth recording. Very early in the life of the LRDG, then called LRP (Long Range Patrol), there was a popular desire for a distinctive badge. So in September 1940, I designed a badge with the help of Dr Edmundson, our doctor of the group. The badge was, however, forbidden for security reasons by Colonel Bagnold. However, I then made a compromise with authority and we had some 100 badges struck as souvenirs to be sent home for keepsakes for our dependants. Colonel Bagnold himself bought one of these.
>
> About a year later, I was bitten three times by a scorpion while on duty at Tazerbo in Libya. The scorpion died and I put it in spirit. From this specimen I designed the present badge of a scorpion within a wheel, and after many requests it was finally adopted and worn as an official badge.

The LRP badge was silver and stamped on the reverse with two or three Arab hallmarks and manufactured by a Cairo jeweller. It was brooch-mounted and exhibited a fat scorpion within a circle that represented a wheel. Grimsey was a competent artist. So when Dr Edmundson asked him to make a design using a scorpion as a symbolic emblem of the desert, he had actually never seen a real one up to that time. Consequently, he copied a poor illustration of an example he saw in a dictionary. Hence the 'fat' scorpion, which was also referred to as the 'scarab' badge as it looked similar to the beetle. Originally the scorpion was gilded with a gold wash. However, with most examples seen today, the gold wash has worn off. Close to 100 badges were struck for the LRP men to purchase before they destroyed the die themselves.

However, by early 1942 the LRDG was finally issued with a cap badge and shoulder titles. Gunner Grimsey also designed the official brass LRDG cap badge, some of which were also made in bronze or blackened brass. The scorpion was now more accurately represented, with the LRDG letters enclosed within the circle. At first consideration was given to including a crown on top, but the idea was discarded in favour of the clean circle. Most of these were produced in Egypt, where they were either cast or die-struck and then hand-cut. There was usually no maker's mark and the quality, finish and design varied. Some examples displayed slightly different patterns on the back of the scorpion. Moreover, the circle varied in form, either being oval or flat with a single or double raised edge. The Cairo jewellers also offered other LRDG-related items such as ashtrays, cigarette cases, rings, lapel and tie pins, plus silver and gold

LRDG 'sweetheart' badges. One badge was even made of gold and studded with diamonds.

The usual shoulder title was a fabric slip-on type with woven red letters onto a navy blue to black background. As they were hand-made by tailors in Cairo, the letter stitching always varied slightly in shape and style. For the New Zealanders and Rhodesians, their national title could be incorporated as well.

The post-war British, Rhodesian and New Zealand LRDG Associations also produced their own individual blazer badges, neck ties and tie and lapel pins. Also a variety of display LRDG badges was produced for mounting on member's vehicles.

LRP R Patrol members dressed like vagrants against the cold. Their truck is covered in a camouflage of hessian scrim cloth.

In the early days of the LRP the wearing of helmets was more common, in line with the regular army, but after a time on long patrols operating in trying conditions the men soon discarded them. They were considered too hot and uncomfortable for regular wear. The helmets were carried in the trucks, but usually only worn when under attack.

G Patrol members keep warm in their issue sheepskin coats, early 1941. The men are all wearing their tinted sand goggles as protection against the dust and sun.

G2 Patrol members, summer 1942. They wear a typical mix of patrol uniform and headdress.

Troopers dressed for the winter. They wear layers of clothing under their greatcoats.

(**Above**) T Patrol LRDG on parade at Abbassia army barracks, 1941. Their formal headdress was the Arab *keffiyeh*. Behind them is the Ford F30 Bofors truck. From right: Trooper R.J. Moore DCM, Trooper L.A. McIver (later died as a PoW), Gunner E.C. Stutterd, Trooper B.F. Shepherd, Corporal D.M. Bassett, unidentified, Trooper R.F. White.

(**Opposite, above**) T2 Patrol. Note the variety of dress and head wear.

(**Opposite, below**) A silver LRP die-struck badge. More than ninety were produced as 'sweetheart' badges to mark the end of the LRP and the beginning of the LRDG in November 1940. Note the Arabic silver hallmarks on the reverse of the LRP badge.

(10)
ACTIVE SERVICE CLOTHING SCALE.

ARTICLE.	Winter scale.	Summer scale.	Weight. lbs.	Price	Remarks
Laces, leather	1	1	-	/-½	-
Shirts, angola	2	-	-	10/-	-
Shoes, canvass	1	1	-	-	-
Shirts, K.D. or Bush.	-	2	-	3/10 (Bush when K.D. run out)	-
Socks, worsted	3	3	-	1/11	-
Towels, hand.	2	2	-	1/6	-
Wallet A.G.	1	1	-	-	-
Hosetop.	-	2	-	1/11	-
Vests cotton	2	2	-	1/11	-

To be maintained out of Special Allowance under War Clothing Regulations, 1941, Para 20.

Brushes, shaving	1	1	-	1/2	-
" hair	1	1	-	2/6	-
" tooth	1	1	-	/5	-
Combs, hair	1	1	-	/2	-
Razor, safety	1	1	-	/5½	-
Soap, cakes	1	1	-	-	-

L.R.D.G. Special Issue.

Gloves, M.T.	1	1	-	8/6	Drivers.
Goggles, M.T.	1	1	-	3/6	Patrol personnel.
Head Dress	1	1	-	69F	-
Chapplies.	1	1	-	-	-
Glasses, sun	1	1	-	-	-
Sheepskin coat or jerkin.	1	-	12	£3	-
Mosquito net	1	1	-	-	-
Blankets.	4	2	5	-	-
Ground sheet	1	1	3	-	-

Copy of an original 1941 document, 'Active Service Clothing Scale'. It shows the regular army clothing issue, plus the special issue for LRDG troops.

Size comparison between left, the official brass LRDG badge (33mm diameter), an LRP lapel pin and LRP badge.

LRDG badge painted by Gunner C.O. 'Bluey' Grimsey. He was very artistic and created the design. He was also an R Patrol navigator until captured in December 1942.

(**Above, left**) Three styles of original LRDG badge. Top: a later-pattern brass die-struck badge and a cast example. Bottom: a silver 'sweetheart' badge. (**Above, right**) Reverse of LRDG badges. The bottom badge is hallmarked and stamped 'silver'.

Size comparison between top, NZ LRDG Association badge, LRDG badge and LRDG tie pin.

Trooper A.M. Saunders displays his LRP badge on his 'Lemon Squeezer' hat. The badge was unofficial and not intended to be worn on uniform.

Second Lieutenant R.J. Landon-Lane wears the RTR (Royal Tank Regiment) Pattern black beret displaying the LRDG badge. By 1943, this pattern beret had replaced the *keffiyeh* as the official LRDG headdress.

(**Left**) Three styles of LRDG shoulder titles: red letters against a navy blue to black title. They were usually hand-woven in Egypt, so there was always a slight variation in the size and weave of the letters. (**Right**) Officers' slip-on shoulder titles, along with a pair of thin LRDG titles.

 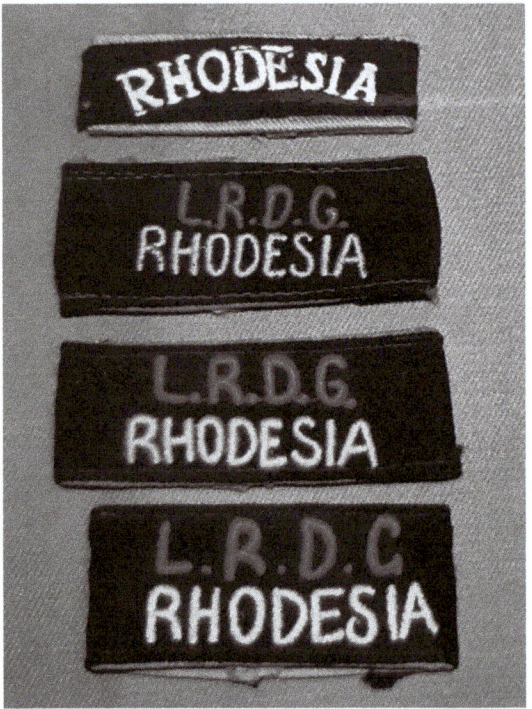

(**Left**) Slip-on titles including 'NZ'. If not done by the Cairo tailors, these could be sown on by the troops themselves. (**Right**) A selection of Rhodesian shoulder titles.

Late-pattern New Zealand LRDG shoulder titles. Below: raiding forces parachuting wings, 1943, from the battledress of Sergeant Merlyn Craw MM.

Trooper R.A. Tippett MM. He wears a German floppy cap as worn by the Ramcke Brigade. They were a Luftwaffe paratrooper unit (*Fallschirmjäger*) who served with the Afrika Korps.

Trooper V.C. Spain with a gazelle that will probably be their next meal of fresh meat. He wears a captured Italian cap.

Trooper I.G. McCulloch wears the issue tinted sunglasses. He also wears the British army issue woollen 'camp comforter' hat. It was popular casual headdress within the patrols.

A souvenir LRP brass ashtray dated 1941.

Trooper F.W. Jopling. His photo appeared as the iconic image of an LRDG 'poster boy', as featured on the cover of *Everybody's Magazine* of 11 October 1941.

Chapter Three

The Vehicles

The first vehicle issue was the 1939 Model Chevrolet WA two-wheel-drive light commercial truck. Bagnold was able to obtain fourteen from the Egyptian army and a further nineteen from a branch of General Motors in Alexandria, possibly 1940 models. To help reduce weight and make them desert-worthy, the windscreens were replaced by aero screens, doors and cab tops removed, springs strengthened with extra leaves and 10.50 × 16 sand tyres fitted, along with various brackets for sun and aero compasses. Gun mountings and sand channels and mats were also installed. Boxes for equipment were fixed to the sides and wireless sets with extra batteries, water containers and condensers for radiators were also added.

In addition, initially seven Ford 01 V8 15cwts were to be used as commanders' pilot cars and as HQ transport. A headquarters unit oversaw the patrols and was supported by a signals, survey and light repair sections. In addition, there was a Heavy Section (trucks for logistical support) that was employed to transport supplies to bases and to establish forward hidden dumps.

With the formation of the LRP it was decided to give the patrol vehicles Maori names beginning with the letter of the patrol: *Rotoma* for R Patrol, *Te Anau* for T Patrol and *Wanaka* for W Patrol. Later when the LRDG was formed, the Guards, Rhodesians and Yeomanry patrols also personalized their vehicles with names.

After about nine months of operations, the reliable but now well-worn and high-mileage Chevrolet WA 30cwt trucks were replaced by an issue of seventy-seven Ford V8 F30 4 × 4 30cwts. However, in January 1941 as an interim measure ten captured Italian Auto-Saharan Company SPA AS37 30cwt four-wheel-drive trucks were also introduced for desert training and evaluation purposes. However, after some employment with the patrols they were not considered suitable for the rigours of LRDG work.

With the new Ford F30s, the radiator grills and vehicle bonnets were removed to assist with cooling and to enable ready access to the radiator and engine. Being four-wheel-drive, they were much heavier than the Chevrolet WA and used twice as much fuel, drastically reducing the effective range of a patrol. Quartermasters had to take special account of supplies required for a trip to allow for the additional petrol to be carried. Water and rations had to be carefully calculated in relation to the proposed distance of travel. Consequently the vehicles became overloaded, resulting in tyres blowing more often and so requiring extra spares to be carried. It also meant that, depending on the mission, the Heavy Section had to establish more forward fuel dumps to accommodate the F30s.

The patrols became the masters of 'behind-the-lines' desert operations, and in addition to their normal reconnaissance work they developed a more aggressive role. Their vehicles mounted a variety of heavy and light machine guns and the Ford F30s continued to carry the 37mm Bofors anti-tank gun.

While the Chevrolets were more popular than the Fords, they were also considered the better vehicle for desert work. Although the four-wheel-drive in the Ford could be useful at times, they were slower and prone to overheating, leading to increased water consumption. Another issue was the placement of the V8 motor, which was mounted between the driver and the front passenger. This meant that it could get very hot and also made it awkward to work on in a hurry. Sergeant R.W.N. Lewis of T1 Patrol wrote in his diary of the problems they were having with their new trucks while on a trip to Kufra:

> 16/04/1941: The V8 Fords are giving a lot of trouble. By the second day four of the batteries had gone flat and there was trouble with some of the gear-boxes. The trucks are sticking a lot and having various mechanical problems. Besides the batteries, tie-rods are bending and one steering box has broken. But they certainly get a thrashing, loaded to top capacity and driven over all different types of going.

The difficulties with the Ford F30 were also highlighted in 1941 by Lieutenant Colonel Bagnold in his LRDG Situation Report Ref: CRME/12785/5/G(5):

> The successes of the Long Range Desert Group last year were due largely to the excellence of the 30cwt Chevrolet trucks, which I had managed to obtain from the Egyptian army. These are now worn out and have been replaced by 30cwt four-wheel-drive Fords, which I was forced to accept without trial.
>
> The Fords have already developed so many defects that the average day's run by a patrol is reduced from 200 miles to 100 miles. The heavy petrol consumption has reduced the self-contained mileage from 1,600 miles to 800 miles. Moreover, the trucks are unsuitable for crossing the great dune areas of which much of inner Libya consists.

In September 1941 a new vehicle was trialled by the LRDG: an American M3A1 open-topped armoured car. It was known in Commonwealth service as a White Scout car and sent to Kufra for evaluation in desert work. A machine gun was also provided so that tests could be made of the rail and skid mountings that were a feature of the vehicle. However, it was found unsuitable for LRDG requirements.

The Ford 01 V8 15cwt pilot cars were wearing out and had been found unsuitable owing to the continual breakage of rear axles that seemed to occur about every 320 kilometres. These vehicles now needed to be replaced and were returned to HQ for base transport. As a further addition to the fleet, eight short-wheel-based Ford F8s were supplied for a time. These were adopted as command cars and often referred to as the 'baby Fords'. By December 1941, both these vehicle types were replaced by twenty-five Chevrolet 1311X3 4 × 2 15cwts obtained from India. They were useful utility trucks and were employed as both command and general-purpose light transport. They were used for only a few months until July 1942, when the LRDG ordered twenty-five American Willys MB 5cwt jeeps to be used as pilot vehicles and HQ transport. In most LRDG official reports, the jeeps were described as 'Bantams' or Willys Bantams. Later in January 1943 a further thirty-one jeeps were ordered to replace vehicle losses.

In March 1942, to replace the Ford F30s, a consignment of specially-ordered and desert-adapted Canadian Chevrolet 1533X2 4×2 trucks had arrived. Originally, 200 trucks were requested but only 112 were ever delivered, the balance thought to have been lost at sea. Though they were only two-wheel-drive, an extra low ratio of gears with a six-cylinder engine producing lower fuel consumption made them ideal for desert work. The patrols now operated as four to five trucks, depending on the mission, led by the commander's jeep.

With the new Chevrolets, they progressed to mounting heavier armament with greater firepower, which increased their offensive capability. The cumbersome heavy Bofors gun was discarded and replaced by the more versatile Italian semi-automatic 20mm Breda Model 35 gun. This was mounted on a carriage turntable, bolted through the rear deck onto the truck chassis. Operated by a crew of two, they fired a twelve-round clip and proved to be a very effective and dependable weapon. One was attached to each patrol.

Each vehicle usually carried a crew of three: the truck commander, a driver and a gunner, who may have also been a cook or medical orderly. The truck commander was responsible for the packing of the interior of the truck, including knowing the contents and the placement of every case and reporting the quantities on board to the patrol leader. He also had to maintain a constant lookout for enemy aircraft and ground forces, as well as keeping station and passing on movement orders to the driver. In addition, he was also responsible for the tactical handling and extraction of his vehicle if it became stuck.

The driver, on the other hand, was responsible for the whole of his truck except the interior of the body which included all the tools and fittings, apart from armament. He had to keep his truck mobile at all times by ensuring regular maintenance such as checking the oil, water and tyre pressures. With the heavy loads, tyre pressure checks were very important and were conducted at every halt. Air was provided by a hose attached to an automatic air pump run from the vehicle's engine. The drivers also had to be alert to the avoidance of hitting rocks and getting stuck in the sand. The selection of the actual track lay directly with him, but the patrol commander was primarily responsible for maintaining the correct speed and direction.

The gunner was not only responsible for the care and maintenance of all armament and munitions, but also to be available to assist with any other general duties as directed by the commander. Every patrol member was trained to be a competent gunner, including the medical orderlies. All crew members were expected to be able to take over each other's responsibilities if required.

Major D.G. (Don) Steele, Commanding Officer of A (NZ) Squadron LRDG, was based at Siwa in late 1941. In 1949 he wrote his LRDG recollections for the NZ War History Branch archive. He reflected on what LRDG trucks had to endure that contributed to their wear and tear and the good work of the fitters:

> A good word should be said about our trucks, they earned it. They were ordinary commercial-type Chevrolets with a few modifications for our special needs. They had the most gruelling time of it in the desert. There were no roads and they spent their lives hauling us over the roughest country for thousands of miles. In this area the shortest trip usually averaged about 500 miles and included every type of desert country, steep hills, rough rocks, dry watercourses, sand and dust. In the winter there was often mud and deep streams or flooded wadis. All this and more, and they never let us down. It is hard for people used to treating their cars humanely to realize just what those trucks had to put up with.
>
> After the most ordinary patrol both the men and trucks had to have a spell. While the men could have doubtless stood a great deal more, it was a most wearing business on the nerves. As soon as the trucks returned, they were stripped of all their guns and equipment and run along to the fitters. There they received all the loving attention that could be lavished on them. Our fitters were probably the best to be found in the Middle East, and they gave their best. It was a matter of pride with them to have the vehicles back on the road with the least possible delay. They would often work right through the night to have a patrol ready for its next task. We owed them a lot!

Staff Sergeant A.F. (Archie) McLeod, who was in charge of the LRDG workshops, gave an overview of the performance of the vehicles. This was recorded by WO2 R.L. Kay, NZ Official Archives, at HQ LRDG on 3 May 1943:

> The four-wheel-drive Fords were used for about 12 months when the LRDG was unable to obtain Chevs. The Chevrolet is a more reliable and faster vehicle in the desert. Although A (NZ) Squadron drivers prefer Chevs, B Squadron prefers Fords. The Chev engines do on average 12,000 to 16,000 miles in the patrol trucks. The fuel consumption varies considerably according to the type of country in which the patrols operate. Over fair going, a good truck can average 50–60 miles an hour in the desert. On average, each truck has a complete overhaul and is re-equipped every six months. Some of the trucks that the LRDG are using at present have been running for 13 to 14 months, but all of these have had their engines replaced. These trucks, however, have passed their best performance.
>
> We started using jeeps when the LRDG was at Kufra in December 1942. We only had two at that stage; now half the vehicles in the LRDG are jeeps. There are twenty-six alone in A Squadron. Before we began using jeeps, each patrol had five 30cwt trucks, but at the moment the conditions have changed

and the 30cwt is no longer a good proposition, so each patrol is entitled to six jeeps. Being a 30cwt vehicle with a 3-ton chassis, the Chev can carry from 2 to 2.5 tons in the desert, but for patrol purposes the jeep's load is estimated to be about 800lb. The squadrons, however, will keep the larger vehicles for workshops, headquarters and that type of work. In the workshops, for instance, there is a machinery lorry, breakdown lorry, four 3-tonners and a 15cwt truck.

The trucks could suffer considerable wear and tear when they undertook topographical reconnaissance missions or 'recce' trips. These journeys involved travelling over new ground, breaking trails and assessing the 'going'. For example, in January 1943 R2 Patrol was assisting Y1 and G2 Patrols in a topographical 'going map' exercise. They set out with two officers, thirteen other ranks and five 30cwt Chevrolet trucks. Operation Report No. 56 describes the task, but what is of particular interest is the series of breakdowns they suffered due to the rough nature of the country. The following is an extract from a report by Sergeant C. Waetford describing the mechanical issues they encountered. They had set out from Zella on 27 December 1942 and returned to Hon on 20 January 1943:

> On 28 December it was necessary to send back to Zella for a new gearbox for R12. On 1 January 1943 we were delayed for 7 hours with repairs to R10's sump. On 4 January, while awaiting instructions from G Patrol, we repaired less serious defections, such as springs, centre bolts, steering boxes, etc. On 10 January, one truck became unserviceable; it took 6 hours to repair. Listed below are the vehicle defects encountered on this trip: 17 × springs, 12 × U-bolts, 5 × steering boxes, 10 × shackles and pins, 1 × radiator, 2 × engines to be changed, 2 × engines to have valve grinds, 2 × defective gearboxes, 2 × track rods, 2 × hangers and bearings, 6 × tyres and tubes, 10 × kingpins and 1 × speedometer.

Driving the heavily-loaded vehicles in a variety of desert conditions required great skill and care, and there were many accidents during the desert war. One example was recorded in the LRDG Operation Report No. 69 by Lieutenant J.D. Henry of S2 Patrol on 28 November 1942. They were working with the Free French Forces at the time:

> S12 [Breda gun truck] developed a bad skid on treacherous surface and on avoiding a palm tree, hit another tree. Damaged radiator, wing and bent chassis. Signalman B.C. Jordan, who was in the truck, was taken to hospital. Enquired about accident, i.e. interviewed driver, passengers and examined the scene of the accident.
> The finding: Truck was travelling at about 15 mph. Crash not due to carelessness – driver not to blame, and Jordan's injuries due to his own

action of jumping from the truck in the wrong direction. He [Jordan] mentioned this in his statement, at the same time exonerating the driver from all responsibility and blame. Medical diagnosis on Jordan: 'Badly sprained ankle and badly bruised; absolute rest for ten days before resuming duty.' Request made for a French signaller to replace Jordan until his recovery.

The Breda truck spent three days in the workshops undergoing repair. Meanwhile, in hospital it was later found that Jordan had suffered a more serious injury, a fractured pelvis. So it was decided to transfer him to the French hospital at Fort Lamy that had better medical facilities. Sadly what was initially thought to be a minor injury developed complications and Signalman Jordan died on 13 December 1942 and was buried at Fort Lamy.

In desert warfare a great risk to all vehicles on both sides was land mines. The LRDG used to lay them behind the lines, as did the Axis forces in their front lines. There were a number of LRDG vehicles put out of action with men injured and killed. One account of such an incident was recorded on 1 December 1942 by Second Lieutenant R.A. Tinker of T1 Patrol in Operation Report No. 51 as they were on their way to undertake Road Watch duties:

> On 25/11/42, after travelling about twelve miles, the leading truck T1 ran on to a mine field in a wadi. Trooper P.J. Burke, a passenger in the front of the truck, suffered a broken left leg and the vehicle was damaged beyond repair. Burke was attended to immediately by the medical orderly and all stores, arms and equipment were removed from the damaged vehicle. When this work was completed the patrol moved to a wadi where the loads were redistributed and two trucks despatched to Kufra with the injured man.

Trooper R.C. Davies was in the same patrol and recorded in his diary his observation of the event:

> Early one morning about four days out as we crept out of the dawning to cross an inland road, our leading truck struck an Italian mine which was specifically placed there to catch the LRDG. What a noise! And what a cloud of smoke sailed into the sky – a great signal for any enemy in the vicinity! Hurrah, no one was seriously hurt, but one chap had his ankle busted up, which meant he had to be taken back to Kufra. He was placed on a stretcher and transferred to another truck and we retrieved all the petrol and stores from the wreck. We have to move fast, that cloud of smoke could betray us so we did get moving – smartly. Back into the broken country and into a deep and narrow wadi, there to hide up and be ready for any trouble. Here we reorganized and two trucks were detailed to take the injured man back to safety. The rest of us would continue on. The two trucks set off about 4.00pm and we moved at dusk and had just got under way when the officers spotted one of the two trucks standing still in the distance. We moved over to it and found that one of them had broken down, beyond our repair. That sort of fixed it for our watch mission, so we all moved back some 50 miles the

next morning and again hid up. We had a wireless message to say we were recalled, so leaving the broken-down trucks hidden we set off back. At Tazerbo our Waco plane took the injured chap to Kufra and we followed on the next day.

The damaged truck T1 could not be repaired by the fitters. It was towed to a wadi and hidden for later recovery. Overall this trip resulted in a number of mechanical failures and frequent stops had to be made, mainly due to faulty electrical equipment, carburettors, petrol pumps, transfer cases and gearboxes.

A Chevrolet WA, 37mm Bofors gun truck cresting a dune.

Chevrolet WA 30cwt, *Rotowaro*.

R Patrol members pose in front of their vehicle stuck in the sand before they push it out. Note most of the men are wearing overalls.

R Patrol trucks parked in front of the captured Italian fort at Jalo. *Rotowhero* is in the foreground.

G Patrol WA truck G9 stuck in the sand. Note the wide use of the steel sand channels to try to extract the vehicle.

R Patrol truck *Rotoiti*. Note the Maori Tiki display on the bonnet indicating it was an R Patrol vehicle. As a token protection against air attack, the steel helmet is at the ready beside the driver. This is an early LRP photo, as the crew are still wearing pith helmets as originally issued. These were soon discarded as they became too battered with the rigors of desert travel and action.

R Patrol WA trucks take a rest before their final approach to Cairo following a mission. The pyramids can be seen in the distance. In the foreground is the commander's Ford V8. The troops referred to the wooden framing on the WA trucks as the 'pig pen'.

The rear wheels of the truck are bogged in soft sand. The trooper begins the laborious job of digging out the wheels to place the steel sand channels to assist extraction.

An above view of the back of a WA truck. It has suffered a minor fire that was quickly put out before the risk of exploding fuel and ammunition. This truck mounts a .55 Boys anti-tank rifle mounted on a metal cross bar. Also a .303 Lewis gun is in place on the passenger's side of the truck.

Kufra, 1941. Left: Private J. Bruce, RAMC medical orderly; right, unidentified. The men rest against a Ford 01 V8 named *Hero*.

Major P.A. Clayton's T Patrol Ford *Te Rangi*. Note the T within the diamond sign on the side of the bonnet. This photo was taken during the Fezzan operations in January 1941, where *Te Rangi* and her crew were later captured by the Italians.

Major P.A. Clayton's Ford 01 *Te Rangi* being examined by the Italians. This was taken following an air attack after the battle of Jebel Sherif in January 1941. Clayton and his New Zealand crew, Lance Corporals W.R. Adams and L. Roderick were the first LRDG men captured in North Africa.

A Y Patrol Ford pilot car with its rear wheels completely stuck. The men are digging out the sand ready to place the steel sand channel.

Two T Patrol Ford 01 pilot cars in the foreground with a Ford F30 truck in the rear. Note the large quantity of stores carried.

Fitters undertake a Ford 01 V8 engine removal for repair or replacement.

A wooden beam and manpower were used to lift the engine.

T Patrol Ford 01 on patrol with a Ford F30 truck. Note the distinctive rock formation.

T Patrol Ford *Te Rangi II* at Abbassia barracks in Cairo. The driver is Trooper W.D. Burnnand. Note the contrasting camouflage pattern on the vehicle.

Ford 01 *Te Rangi II* with Trooper W.D. Burnnand at the wheel.

The crashed *Te Rangi II* after flying 18 metres over a razorback dune in 1941. It had to be transported in the back of a Ford F30 to base workshops for repair.

Captain D.G. Steele's Ford *Rotoma* on a halt after a small fire started in the rear. The stores and equipment are being examined and sorted.

A Ford 01 V8 restored as a workshop vehicle for the Light Repair Section, 1943. Left: Corporal H.P. Hewetson and Sergeant W.R. Bambery. Note the scorpion painted on the mudguard.

Y Patrol Ford CMP F8 8cwt 4 × 2 pilot car *Dartagnan* undergoing a wheel change.

A T Patrol Ford F8 leads a column of Ford F30 trucks out on a mission.

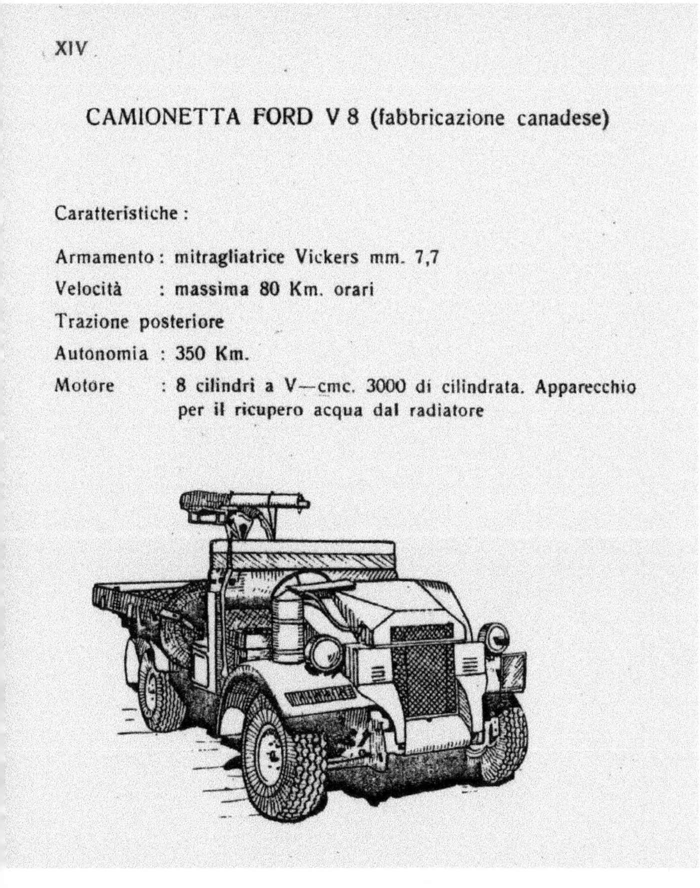

XIV

CAMIONETTA FORD V 8 (fabbricazione canadese)

Caratteristiche :

Armamento : mitragliatrice Vickers mm. 7,7
Velocità : massima 80 Km. orari
Trazione posteriore
Autonomia : 350 Km.
Motore : 8 cilindri a V—cmc. 3000 di cilindrata. Apparecchio per il ricupero acqua dal radiatore

A page from a 1942 Italian military manual identifying British vehicles, *I Mezzi Corazzati Nemici* (*The Enemy Armoured Vehicles*). This illustrates and describes the Ford F8. Interesting that they included this vehicle as only eight were issued to the LRDG and used for just a limited time.

A close-up of the F8 grill of the T1 command vehicle. Note the water condenser on the left.

An F8 (left) and an F30 (right) parked alongside 'the wire'. The F8 command vehicle mounts a .303 Vickers heavy machine gun.

Trooper W.D. Burnnand (left) and Trooper R.J. Moore DCM (right) pose alongside an F8. Note the sand mat rolled up below the Vickers machine gun.

A rear view of the F8. The trooper is unidentified.

Captain L.B. Ballantyne, T Patrol, checks his F8 command car. Standing: Trooper R.J. Moore DCM.

R Patrol Ford F30 at Siwa, 1941. The patrol was identified by a Maori *Tiki* figure painted on the front mudguard, whereas T Patrol displayed a Kiwi. The driver is Trooper A.F. Dodunski; the other men are unidentified.

Trooper D.A. Hutchins poses in front of his Y Patrol F30 truck *Tipperary Tim*.

A Ford F30 totally destroyed after receiving a direct hit from a Junkers Ju 87 Stuka.

(**Above**) Ford F30 *Aramis* of Y Patrol. It is parked next to the Farouk Hotel in Siwa. Left: Trooper B.C. Springford; and back: Trooper A.H. Cave.

(**Opposite, above**) An unusual photo of two R Patrol men peering over the grill of their F30 truck on which a 'V' has been painted.

(**Opposite, below**) A Ford F30 crossing dunes with care. The sand channel is ready for use if required.

(**Above**) A Ford F30 rests on top of a sand dune. Y Patrol Trooper L.S.A. Coombes is on the right.

(**Opposite, above**) T Patrol inspection at the Abbassia barracks in Cairo. All the trucks are Ford F30s.

(**Opposite, below**) R Patrol truck *Rotowhero* with rear wheels deeply stuck in a salt pan. Front two men are, from left: Trooper R.J. Landon-Lane and Private R.H. Tinker.

Trooper L.A. McIver stands in the LRDG garage/workshops at Abbassia, Cairo. Left are Ford F30s, centre a Ford 01 pilot car, and on the right Heavy Section trucks.

A Ford F30 *Te Paki II*. The headlights appear darkened to lessen reflection. The men are dressed for cold weather. Note the Lewis gun resting on the bonnet.

A Ford F30 photographed from another truck.

A Ford F30 travelling at speed on a flat gravel plain or *serir*.

A Ford F30 sunk in a well. Note the stores in the back. The truck still retains its canopy frame. These were soon discarded as they impeded aerial vision.

Two heavily-loaded T Patrol Chevrolet 1533X2 trucks. In March 1942, a shipment of 112 of these vehicles was received by the LRDG. The original order was for 200 vehicles; however, 88 of them were lost at sea.

This R Patrol truck *Rotowai* R4 revs its engine.

R Patrol truck *Rotowaro* R5. Note the Maori *Tiki* painted on the bonnet indicating it is an R Patrol truck. Trooper F.J.W. McKeown stands in front.

TE PAK

TIRAU

TE AROHA III

(**Opposite, above**) Truck parked in a position to blend with the landscape. They always faced outwards to ensure a quick escape if needed.

(**Opposite, below**) A line-up of T1 Patrol Maori truck names.

(**Above**) The hard work of extracting a bogged vehicle. The metal sand tray is at the ready.

S Patrol Breda gun truck S12 after it lost control in a skid and hit a tree. It wrecked its mudguard and radiator, and also bent the chassis. Unfortunately, Signalman B.C. Jordan jumped from the truck when the accident happened and broke his pelvis. He died about two weeks later from complications following his injury.

A heavily-loaded and well-armed Y Patrol truck 'Cock of the North' Y12. It mounts a single .303 Vickers K machine gun and a heavy water-cooled .50 Vickers machine gun in the rear. Note the spare tyre tied to the front bumper.

Y Patrol truck *Chattanooga Choo Choo* Y11 in the foreground. It is rare to see the sand channel mounted in front of the grill. Also, on the right, it was uncommon to have a spare tyre held in a cage over the grill.

Y Patrol truck Y7 deeply embedded in soft sand after crossing a dune.

Crossing a sand sheet at speed. Two Chevrolet 1533X2 trucks have another in tow.

Private A.F. 'Blondie' Goddard, S Patrol, at Siwa. His jeep, S13, mounts twin .303 Vickers K machine guns.

Y Patrol men rest for a meal in a well-concealed position. The LRDG usually referred to their jeeps in their reports as 'Bantams'.

S Patrol jeeps parked up checking equipment. Most of the guns are covered to protect them from the dust. The vehicles are fully loaded with fuel and supplies.

S Patrol column on a halt with the command jeep in the centre.

A command jeep leading a column on an escarpment. Note the spare wheel on the side. It was more common for the spares to be attached to the rear.

A cartoon drawing by Signalman D. Searle of 'Scorpio the Gangster' in his LRDG jeep, 1943.

A Chevrolet 1311X3 4 × 2 15cwt HQ1 at Hon. Left: Captain J.R. Easonsmith, Sergeant Major J. Penfold, Captain W.B. Kennedy Shaw (driver), Corporal E. Gutteridge, Captain D.L. Lloyd Owen, Quartermaster Captain D. Barrett, Captain L.H. Browne and Captain T. Hayward. Twenty-five of these vehicles were issued to replace the Ford 01s and F8s.

(**Above**) An Italian SPA AS37 30-cwt four-wheel-drive on patrol in LRDG use. These were employed for desert training and evaluated for potential patrol use. However, they were found unsuitable for the requirements of LRDG work.

(**Opposite, above**) An American M3A1 open-topped armoured car, also known in Commonwealth service as the White Scout car. One similar to the example shown here was trialled by the LRDG for patrol use, but was found to be unsuitable for their needs.

(**Opposite, below**) A Ford 01 V8 and a Chevrolet CMP C60L 3-ton truck of the Light Repair Section (LRS). It is marked W.S.2 (Workshop) and the truck is named *Beatrice*. Centre: Private N.B. Boyd, a G Patrol fitter and armourer. The other men are unidentified.

Private F.R. McCallum, Light Repair Section, standing in front of a Chevrolet CMP C60L workshop truck. Note the scorpion symbol plate over the headlight space. A headlight has been fixed further below.

Refuelling a Bristol Bombay bomber/transport using flimsy cans of fuel that were carried on the aircraft. Its mission was to rescue survivors of the Barce raid in September 1942 on Landing Ground 125. Centre: Major V. Peniakoff talks to Captain D.L. Lloyd Owen of Y1 Patrol who rendezvoused with the aircraft. A Chevrolet CMP C60L 3-ton truck is parked under the wing to assist with the refuelling.

Chapter Four

The Heavy Section

The primary role of the trucks of the Heavy Section was to establish and provision forward supply dumps. This helped to maintain the Group's long-range capacity and a number of officers took a turn in the Heavy Section. The trucks regularly transported fuel, water, rations, munitions and equipment to forward dumps, or between supply depots to LRDG bases. Often these journeys were adventures in themselves, involving both navigational and heavy vehicle desert driving skills over great distances. With the LRP, the first trucks were four 6-ton Ford Marmon-Herringtons supplied to the unit by the Southern Mediterranean Oil Company. Up to December 1940, the heavy truck section was referred to as the Marmon-Herrington Party. Later these were replaced by four 10-ton Whites and the unit renamed the Heavy Section. In spring 1942, they in turn were replaced by six 10-ton Mack NR9s. Soon after, twenty Ford F60 CMP trucks were added. It was now organized into four detachments known as H.S. 1, 2, 3 and 4. From December 1942 into early 1943, its work included trips from Kufra to Cairo and Tobruk with forward dumping from Hon to points almost as far west as the Tunisian frontier. Their work was not without danger. A tragic loss occurred on 15 January 1943 when the Heavy Section commander Lieutenant P.L. Arnold was killed along with Driver J.H. Gravil when their vehicle ran over an Italian 'coffin' mine near Hon. Arnold was succeeded by Lieutenant A.S. Denniff.

Staff Sergeant A.F. McLeod, who was in charge of the LRDG workshops, described working in the Heavy Section in the early days. This was recorded by WO2 R.L Kay, NZ Official Archives, at HQ LRDG on 3 May 1943:

> I was then a fitter for the Heavy Section, which had two six-wheel-drive Marmon-Herrington lorries and a 30cwt Chev. The Marmon-Herringtons were good vehicles in the desert and could carry about 144 cases of petrol each, as well as their own fuel and spare parts. When one of them was stuck in the sand it was pulled clear by the other.
>
> The first trip I made with a Marmon-Herrington was to Dalla to make a dump for LRDG patrols. On this trip, one vehicle sustained a broken chassis. We repaired this on the spot and returned to Cairo. Altogether, we made three trips to Dalla from Cairo, one to Wadi Halfa and two from Wadi Halfa to the Gilf Kebir plateau. On one of the trips to the Gilf, a Marmon-Herrington cracked a cylinder block; it took us seven or eight hours to repair this in the desert. It was a very difficult job. The next trip we made with these vehicles was to Dalla. We also collected near Uweinat two Fiat diesel trucks

which we had captured from the Italians by one of our patrols. We took them as far as the Gilf and abandoned them there on account of burnt-out clutches. As far as I know they are still there.

We made a trial run with a Mack and White lorry from Cairo to Dalla. We did not carry spare parts with the Mack so had to leave it near Mushroom Rock, about halfway, on account of a broken fan belt. We took the White right to Dallas, however, dumped its load, and returned to Cairo. We returned to collect the Mack, which still had its load, two or three days later. I drove it back myself and made as fast a trip as possible. I do not know how long it took me to drive the White from Dalla to Cairo, a distance of 400 miles, but I am sure it was a record from a heavy vehicle in the desert.

Captain D. Barrett, Quartermaster LRDG, described the maintenance of the LRDG in the field. This was recorded by WO2 R.L Kay, NZ Official Archives, at HQ LRDG on 3 May 1943:

When the LRDG was based at Kufra, we received our supplies from Wadi Halfa; when we were at Siwa we received our supplies from Mersa Matruh; when we were at Jalo we received them from Msus; when we were at Hon we received them from Tripoli and Misurata. Our Heavy Section would bring a month's supply in one trip; this included 12,000 rations [36 tons]. When each patrol was away on a trip, it took a month's supplies with it and we kept a reserve in case it should be necessary to re-equip a patrol upon its return to Group headquarters. We avoided accumulating a particularly large reserve, however, in case we should have to make an unexpected move to a fresh base area. Only at one place, Jalo, did we lose any supplies on this account.

The Heavy Section did not have to make more than one major journey when the LRDG was moving its base from one place to another, such as from Siwa to Kufra. Adequate transport facilities were provided by five 10-ton Mack lorries and twenty-five 3-tonners. Sometimes, however, it was necessary to move supplies by bounds, when the vehicles would dump one load and return for the balance and thus leapfrog forward to the new base.

It was a 1,400-mile haul from Wadi Halfa to Kufra. During much of the time the LRDG was at Kufra the unit was operating behind the enemy lines, but for a week or so, after Rommel had driven westwards from Cyrenaica, the Heavy Section carried supplies from Tobruk to Kufra through the Sand Sea.

In carrying large quantities of petrol across many hundreds of miles of desert, the LRDG could not afford to use leaking containers. From the time jerrycans were introduced to British forces in the Western Desert, the LRDG was able to make good use of these containers. By making dumps of petrol in the desert, 500 to 600 miles from base, the Heavy Section enabled patrols to operate over a greater radius.

While operating in Libya, the LRDG was absolutely self-contained and maintained its own vehicles. At no time since February 1941 have we not had at least one squadron in the field. The patrols used to return to Cairo every six months for a complete refit and overhaul. This also enabled men to go on leave after long periods in the desert.

In addition to the Heavy Section, a small section of 3-tonners was sometimes required to get advance or urgent requirements from Cairo, such as guns and motor transport requirements. The Group was never really seriously short of supplies, although on one occasion at Zella, when six trucks were delayed for a week, supplies were reduced to a minimum of two days' reserve. Usually the Heavy Section maintained a regular schedule and ran to a reliable timetable.

An example of a typical Heavy Section operation is outlined in the LRDG Operational Instruction No. 81 dated 17 January 1943. The H.S.2 commander was Captain A. Denniff with seven other ranks travelling in three Ford F60 3-ton trucks. Their task was to transport 5,300 litres of petrol, in the best time possible, to a site named Wilder's Dump. The load consisted of 480 jerrycans of petrol and twenty-one days of rations and water. In addition, they were to carry truck spares for T1 Patrol to be left at the dump or given to them if met. The parts consisted of U-bolts, centre bolts and front and rear springs.

The trucks were armed with the following weapons: one pair Vickers K, two single Vickers K, one .50 Vickers and a .300 Breda. With such a combustible load of fuel being transported, the small column would be very vulnerable if subject to enemy ground or air attack.

The instructions prepared by Lieutenant Colonel G. Prendergast, Commander LRDG, were as follows and were successfully accomplished without incident:

> You will proceed to the dump area by a route to be obtained from the Intelligence Officer. You will also obtain from him details of the enemy and own troop movements in the vicinity of your route. You will signal your position, without fail, each day, and will inform this HQ the astro-fix position of the dump, together with a description of any prominent landmarks to facilitate recognition of the dump. If for any reason you are unable to communicate with this HQ, you will make the dump at exactly Q.T. 5010, at which point you will await the arrival of T1 Patrol, who will be ordered to meet you there. If this point is unsuitable for a dump, you will then go with T1 Patrol and make the dump at a more suitable place and return to Hon with T1 Patrol.

The Heavy Section H.S.2 departed on 17 January 1943 and returned to Hon on 27 January 1943. The only problem was a faulty speedo cable in one of the trucks that took a morning to rectify.

LRP Heavy Section trucks being transported by train, Cairo 1940.

Ford Marmon-Herrington trucks parked in the desert.

LRP Heavy Section members. Note the rum jars in front. From left: Sergeant A.W. Hood, unidentified, Private A.F. McLeod, Trooper J. Zimmerman, Lance Corporal J.L. Schaab, unidentified, nickname 'Midnight'. Front left: unidentified, Lieutenant C.A. Holliman, Private E.T. Russell.

Heavy Section men feeding a migrating bird that stopped for a drink.

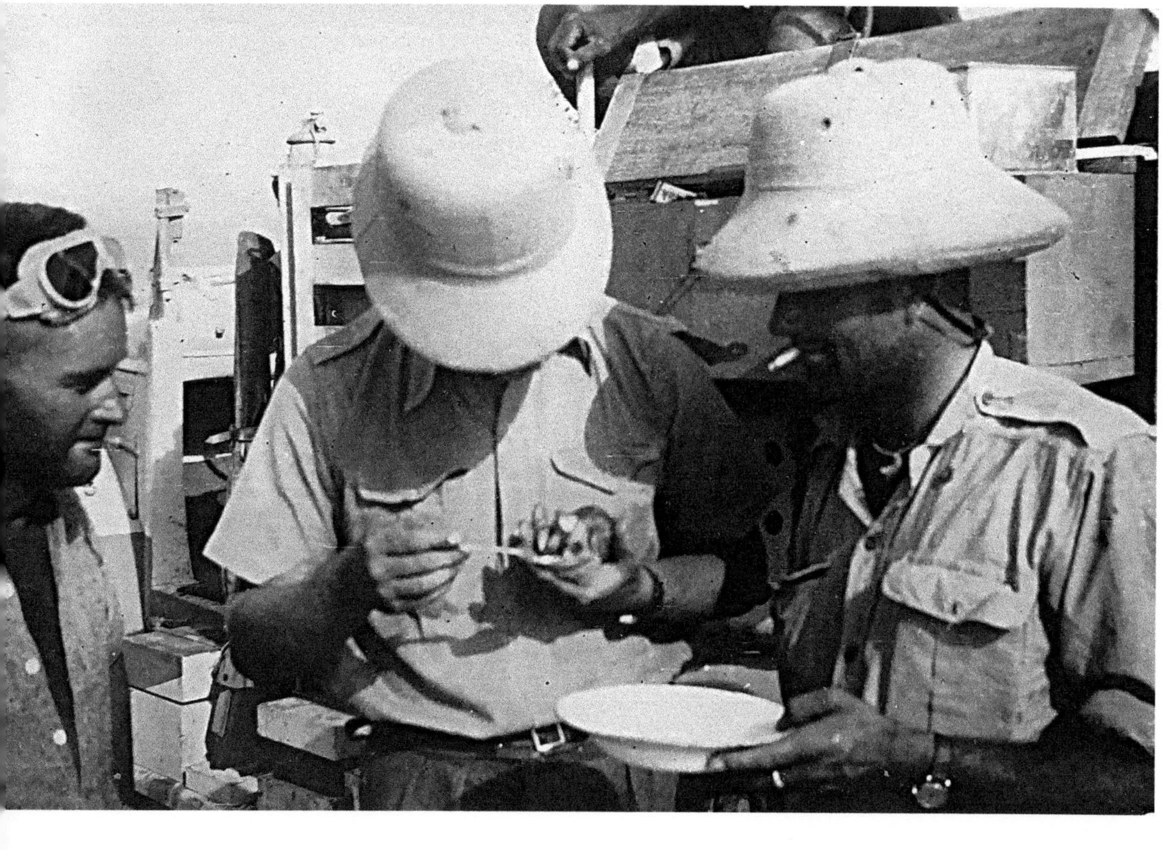

A bogged Marmon-Herrington truck, 1940. It carried a heavy load of petrol for a dump at Ain Dalla, Egypt.

A rear view of the same truck. Note the distinctive camouflage pattern.

The Marmon-Herrington Heavy Section Chevrolet WA HQ command car named *Matai*. Note the contrasting camouflage pattern.

Heavy Section Ford F60 truck stuck in the sand.

A Ford F30 is loaded in the back of the Heavy Section White truck HS4.

Captain P.L. Arnold, Heavy Section commander, rests beside his truck. He was later killed on 15 January 1943 when his vehicle ran over a land mine near Hon.

Heavy Section Mack NR9 10-ton truck.

A mix of Heavy Section and Ford F30 patrol vehicles halts on a desert plain. In the foreground is a Ford F60 3-ton truck.

On the left are a Heavy Section Ford F60 and a Chevrolet 1311X3 15cwt pilot car mounting a Vickers K on the right.

Chapter Five

Navigation

Accurate navigation was essential for both desert survival and to the success of a mission. The absence of recognizable landmarks made it necessary for the patrols to navigate as if by sea: by compass, the sun and stars. Every truck was equipped with either a sun, aero or magnetic compass. They also carried maps of their transit and operating areas so that they could get home independently if required.

Navigation in the desert had two parts: a 'dead reckoning' course by sun compass and speedometer and an 'astro-fix' by observations of the stars with a theodolite to check the accuracy of the 'D.R.' position. In dead reckoning, a line from the point of departure to the objective was ruled on the map. The patrol followed the general direction of that line, but deviated from time to time as required by the terrain and other considerations. The navigator recorded the times, sun compass bearings and the distance travelled on each bearing by speedometer reading and plotted the data on the map at each halt. The final point on the map arrived at by that method was the 'dead reckoning position'.

Each patrol had a senior navigator who plotted the course and compared it with a second check navigator who travelled in a different vehicle. As soon as it was dark the navigator, with his Star Atlas by his side, set up his theodolite and 'shot' the stars. First an assistant noted the sixth 'pip' of the Greenwich time signal with his stop-watch, then with the aid of a timekeeper who noted the exact second, detailed readings of certain stars were recorded, after which some time was spent trying to convert the readings to longitude and latitude to establish a position. This was done with reference to the astronomical navigation tables. It was often a struggle in the chill and dark of a desert evening to try to work out the complex calculations. The result was then reported to the patrol commander. The navigator usually travelled in the wireless truck behind the commander's vehicle.

Trooper (later Lieutenant) R.F. (Frank) White wrote of his navigation experiences:

> At night you could drive navigating by the stars. You used to set up your theodolite and shoot yourself in. One fellow one night shot himself in the middle of the Indian Ocean! What you did, you set it on a certain star which you knew, you had a fellow on the wireless which was tuned into Greenwich Mean Time and you would say 'Coming up, coming up, coming up, up.' Directly you said 'Up', he had to have the time. Then you took another star

and you did exactly the same thing. Then you had all the times and everything and the tables told you where the two lines crossed.

The Italian maps were shocking! Six to eight miles out at the least. So we navigated by sun compass. We had Air Force Navigation Tables to work from for each month. The stylus on top of the compass showed the shadow and the tables told you how much to turn it around, so that you could drive in a straight line or so for a hundred miles all day by just following the shadow. It was really quite a simple way.

The LRDG became the Middle East experts in navigation. Bagnold wrote two military training manuals on the subject. Also Group members sometimes conducted courses on navigation for the officers and men from units of the Eighth Army. The skill of the work was recognized in 1942 when the War Office approved a new army trade, Land Navigator, earning extra pay of 1 shilling per day.

Another important task was topographical reconnaissance missions. This was to report the nature of the landscape known in the LRDG as 'the going' for the creation of a 'going map'. This would describe main obstacles, accessibility, cover, wadi crossings, scarps and possible lines of march, along with water supplies such as wells and springs. Furthermore, it would report on areas with prominent landmarks for navigation that were suitable for landing grounds with little work needed and did not require graders. By January 1943 all LRDG patrols were engaged under the command of the Eighth Army to obtain information for the making of 'going maps'. It was considered a priority job and the LRDG was taken off all other work to complete it.

Major D.G. Steele recorded his thoughts on these operations:

> A favourite job the Army had for us, though not very popular with us, was 'Going Recce'. We would be asked to find out if a force of all arms could travel from point A to point B. We would then have to plod over the route indicated, imagining we were tanks or armoured cars or army lorries with a lot of bloody fools sitting behind the wheel, making notes all the way on the nature of the surface and gradients etc. Still, these recces were nearly mostly in safe country and so in a way were a rest from worrying about the enemy.

It was interesting what was discovered on these trips which the LRDG described in their reports as a 'recce'. An example is from the Operation Report No. 61 dated 12 November 1942. Lieutenant J. Henry of S2 Patrol recorded, apart from topographical findings, what he had come across while on a recce in the El Agheila-Marada area. They were travelling in five patrol trucks and two HQ trucks carrying eighty cases of spare petrol. Extracts from the report are as follows:

> 29 October: Found wrecked British plane [assumed to be a Beaufighter], twin-engined and the remains of two bodies [a pilot officer and a sergeant].

The plane was in pieces, spread over 300–400 yards. The bodies that had been mauled by bird and beast were buried.

The remains of two unopened parachutes were also found. Numbers and letters FMA.3671 DRG 9747/3 were found on a plate on the wing. Wireless serial No. 3063. No articles for identification purposes were found near the Pilot Officer. The Sergeant's wallet and pay book were discovered. Probable date of crash September 1941.

3 November: Reached enemy landing ground. It is at least one square mile in extent. Surface hard sand. Found one 44-gallon drum of Italian aviation spirit and a 44-gallon drum of water. We left the water, but took the aviation spirit. Took an astro-fix of the ground.

5 November: Camped near a pool of standing water. Saw six camels in vicinity of pool branded with U.I.V.I. on their necks. Found camel saddle containing articles of Italian uniform. No papers etc. Probably stolen by local natives. No signs of owner except recent fire place and footprints.

One of the last significant desert actions of the Group was supporting the Eighth Army advance into Tunisia. In preparation for this, it was required to reconnoitre and map the country's southern approaches through which a column would have to pass, outflanking the Axis-held Mareth Line. In January and February 1943, the LRDG and Indian Long Range Squadron explored the territory to the south and the west of the range of hills extending southwards from Matmata. As they progressed the patrols signalled HQ daily, reporting the 'going', obstacles, cover, water supply and sites for landing grounds. On their return the commanders conferred with LRDG Intelligence Officer Captain L.H. Browne at the NZ Division HQ, where a model was made to demonstrate possible lines of advance.

On 12 January, T1 Patrol under Captain N.P. Wilder crossed the frontier and became the first troops of the Eighth Army to enter Tunisia. They found an uncharted pass south through the Matmata Hills, which became known as Wilder's Gap. It was by this route two months later that the NZ Division executed its 'left hook' round the fortified Mareth Line. Other patrols explored the country further to the west. T2 investigated the area to the south of Djebel Tebaga between Matmata and Chott el Djerid, a high salt marsh, while G2 explored the area between the Chott and the Grand Erg Oriental, which was an impassable sand sea that extended into southern Algeria.

While on this topographical mission, T2 Patrol under Lieutenant R.A. Tinker accompanied by Major V. Peniakoff and his men of Popski's Private Army set up a base camp south of Ksar Rhilane. From there Tinker and Peniakoff, each in a small party of two jeeps, went north towards Djebel Tebaga where a natural corridor extended to the Matmata Hills towards the coast at Gabes. This was the Tebaga Gap through which the outflanking of the Mareth Line was to be done. After a time the men parted company to continue with separate tasks: the PPA to carry out demolitions in the Matmata area and T2 to map the 'going' in the direction of Chott el Djerid. While they were away, the main body of the LRDG and PPA patrols camped at Ksar Rhilane to await the return of the jeep section. Lance Corporal R.C. (Ron) Davies was with T2 patrol and wrote a diary account of what happened to him after their base camp was attacked by enemy fighter aircraft on 27 January 1943:

> On the radio we heard that Tripoli had been taken, so that night we had a double ration of rum to celebrate. Two days later, two of our vehicles set off to reconnoitre the Mareth Line area and we settled down to a three-day wait. Breakfast was at an easy hour the next morning and just as we were finishing at 8.25am, two ME 109s [Messerschmitt Bf 109Fs] flew over to our left at 200ft. We kept awfully still and when they had gone there was much talk! What on earth were planes doing in our isolated area? The trucks were in a wadi and semi-camouflaged. We decided to leave them that way and to also cover the guns and lay low hoping that Jerry wouldn't see us. Five minutes later the two planes flew back coming straight towards our camp. One circled over us and then they came right in! Alas! My beautiful .5 cannon was away with the other two trucks so I couldn't hit back. When I saw one fighter coming for our truck I ducked behind the wheel and felt the whole earth quiver as cannon shells smashed into the truck. I was unfortunate to have my leg sticking out and got bits of cannon shrapnel that went through my calf and some came out of my shin. Things weren't looking so good, so I hopped away into a short wadi in the bank and there stayed and watched the Jerries get all our trucks [four LRDG and three PPA vehicles]. Some of the chaps managed to get their guns going, but it was useless. However, the Huns did a good job – for themselves. They ran out of ammo in getting the last truck and cleared off and wasn't there a sigh of relief all round! It had been rather a hectic ten minutes and reminded me intensely of Crete.
>
> One of the trucks wasn't burning very badly and we threw some petrol cans and explosives off it and then tried to start it. No good, a burst had gone right into the engine. So we threw off two boxes of rations and some water. After having my wound dressed by the medical orderly with us, who also did up the other chap who was wounded [Lance Corporal R.A. (Dick) Ramsay], we had a quick conference and decided to make off into the sand dunes as there would surely be a ground patrol out looking for us. We decided that an Arab agent of the Germans had given us away, probably by wireless, and this was pretty well confirmed later.
>
> We all got into the sand dunes and lay doggo for the rest of the day. The food was not plentiful and neither was water. It was decided that the only way for us to get out of it was to go to Sabria, a French fort and from there to Tozeur which was to our north-west. It meant a walk of over 200 miles for most of the chaps. That night Popski came back and found out what had happened. All the wireless gear was gone, so we could tell no one of our plight.

At a disused fort – Ksar Rhilane about 20 miles north of us – he had encountered the remnants of a Free French paratrooper unit which had been shot up at Gabes and they decided to fall in with us and try to reach civilization in Tunisia as well. Popski took Dick and me to that fort in the early hours of the following morning and the rest followed on foot. By this time our legs had stiffened and we couldn't walk. Popski gave Dick and me some morphia for the pain. I was away with the fairies and really enjoyed that part.

The paratroopers made us comfy in the fort. I had the officer's bed-roll, and did we sleep! In the morning they fixed us a pretty good breakfast and then we were pretty right. The same day as our walking party arrived, so did our officer and his party got back in their jeeps. Ron Tinker jacked things up very quickly and organized our movement. Just before we left there, the two Hun planes came over the fort and boy! Did we lay low? Did we what! They were on their way home, however, and didn't reappear. It shows that even at that time Jerry was watching the rear of his Mareth positions very closely. Then two of our jeeps and one of Popski's set off for Sabria carrying two wounded and others who were not too good on the walking. The going was terrific of the type of country we travelled over. I was comfy in the jeep though and didn't suffer very much at all. We encountered wandering tribes of natives with their flocks of sheep, goats and whatever a lot of camels are called, and enquired of them regarding the state of affairs in the area we were getting into. When in sight of Sabria a shepherd boy told us it had been bombed and then the garrison had evacuated it, so we had to push on to Nefta. That night we reached Sidi Mursuk and after watching the oasis for some time encouraged a native to go in with us, as he told us there were no Ities there. We told him we'd shoot him if there were. It was ok. We got water there and some filthy dates from the holy man – an old bloke who looked after some tomb or other. Here also we got a native who would guide us to a good road on the edge of the Chott el Djerid. What a ride in the dark that was! There was no road, however – just a camel track! We paid him his 500 lire, however, and camped there for the rest of the night.

The next morning in the bitter cold we set off again and went on as fast as we could in that rotten terrain. We lurched upon a herd of camels and the native in charge gave us a drink of camels' milk which was surprisingly good. It tastes just like coconut milk in fact. I guess we were hungry enough to eat and drink anything though!

Late that afternoon we crossed the edge of the Chott and reached Nefta. The French believed it impossible for vehicles to cross that salt marsh and even though we'd fired Verey lights no one knew we were there until we reached the town square! Were they surprised? Nefta is just like any town in Egypt – the inhabitants mostly natives. However, the French police and some of their wives were there and they did us well! Gave us wine and fried eggs, also bread. The wine on very empty tummies made us feel quite happy!

The police rang through to Tozeur for petrol and a staff car came dashing in about half an hour later full of dapper French officers and petrol. One of Popski's Lts and the French Position officer could wangle the lingo so things were right. We filled up with petrol and in half an hour were in Tozeur – 20 miles away. The road was wonderful to travel on after the desert, believe me. Dick and I were taken straight to the Civil Hospital. The French Doc could speak a little English and it was very funny him asking us questions. 'It is hurt, no? Yes?' He stuck a probe into my leg and I must have gone a bit white for he started to slap me in the face! I nearly gave him one in the jaw before I realized what he was doing. I don't think I was fainting! He wanted us to stay in the hospital, but the only sister there was pretty ancient but very nice – she gave us wine too! We wanted to be with the other chaps so went to where they were billeted. What a hole! The French army doesn't think much of the Kiwi soldier apparently as we were dumped in the same barracks as their native troops! There was a good hotel in the place too. The officers went there and we didn't begrudge them that though. There were First Army rations there for us as our people had provided against this sort of accident occurring. Boy! Their rations were mighty good. Plum pudding, jam pud, date pud, seven Players cigs per man, sweets, chocolate – scotch broth, oxtail soup and tinned veges. We wondered what we had struck. And so to bed on the stone floor and a wonderful night's sleep.

Next morning Ron Tinker took a Jeep and two drivers to Gafsa to get more jeeps to go back to pick up the walking party. However, we couldn't get them there and went on across the border into Tébessa, Algeria, where we got two from the Yanks.

The final task assigned to the LRDG by the Eighth Army was the navigation of the New Zealand Corps during the outflanking of the Mareth Line in March 1943. Appropriately the work was performed by New Zealanders: Captain R.A. Tinker with three men from T2 Patrol in two jeeps, who would be acting as guides. The New Zealand Corps passed through Wilder's Gap and remained at an assembly area, while the route was plotted to the north-west. A wadi with steep rocky escarpments presented a very difficult obstacle but Tinker, accompanied by New Zealand Engineers, found a place where tracks could be constructed with road-making machinery to get heavy transport across.

The Eighth Army launched its frontal attack on the Mareth Line. From there they moved forward to Tebaga along the route reconnoitred by the Group and made contact with the enemy on 21 March. Eventually the Axis forces were driven back to a corner of Tunisia, ending with their final surrender in North Africa on 13 May 1943. The LRDG was released from the Eighth Army only after there was no further scope for them, having 'run out of desert'. They returned to Egypt to rest and reorganize.

Corporal L.H. (Tony) Browne taking a 'shot' with his theodolite. He first joined the LRP as a navigator and after a time was commissioned and became a patrol commander. He served with distinction with the LRDG, earning the DCM, MC and MID.

Private T.E. Ritchie gives his comrade Trooper N.R. Campbell a haircut. In the background a navigational position is being taken using a theodolite.

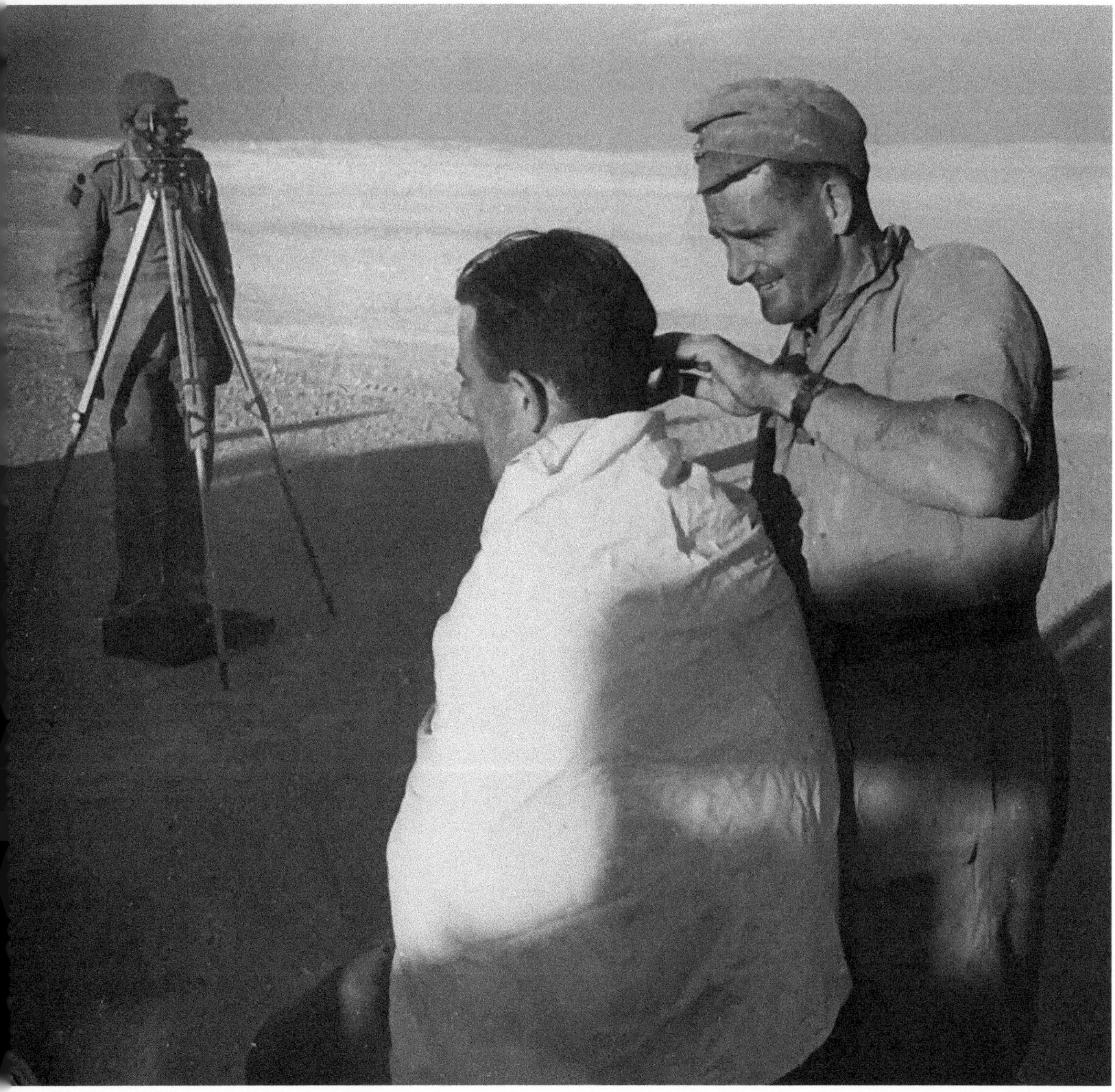

LRP men of R Patrol gather around the 'Big Cairn', 1940. It was erected by Pat Clayton in 1931 as a navigation beacon and was to become an important LRDG staging-point. After crossing over from Egypt, it was placed on a featureless flat sand and gravel plain that extended for several hundred kilometres inside Libya.

(**Left**) *Field Navigation Astro-Fix* training manual (April 1942) and (**Right**) *Elementary Map Reading* military manual (1941).

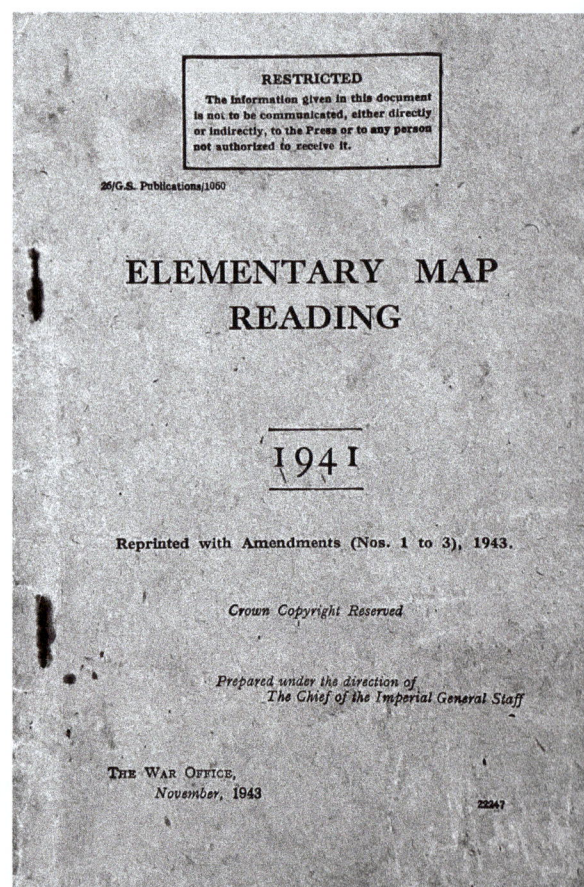

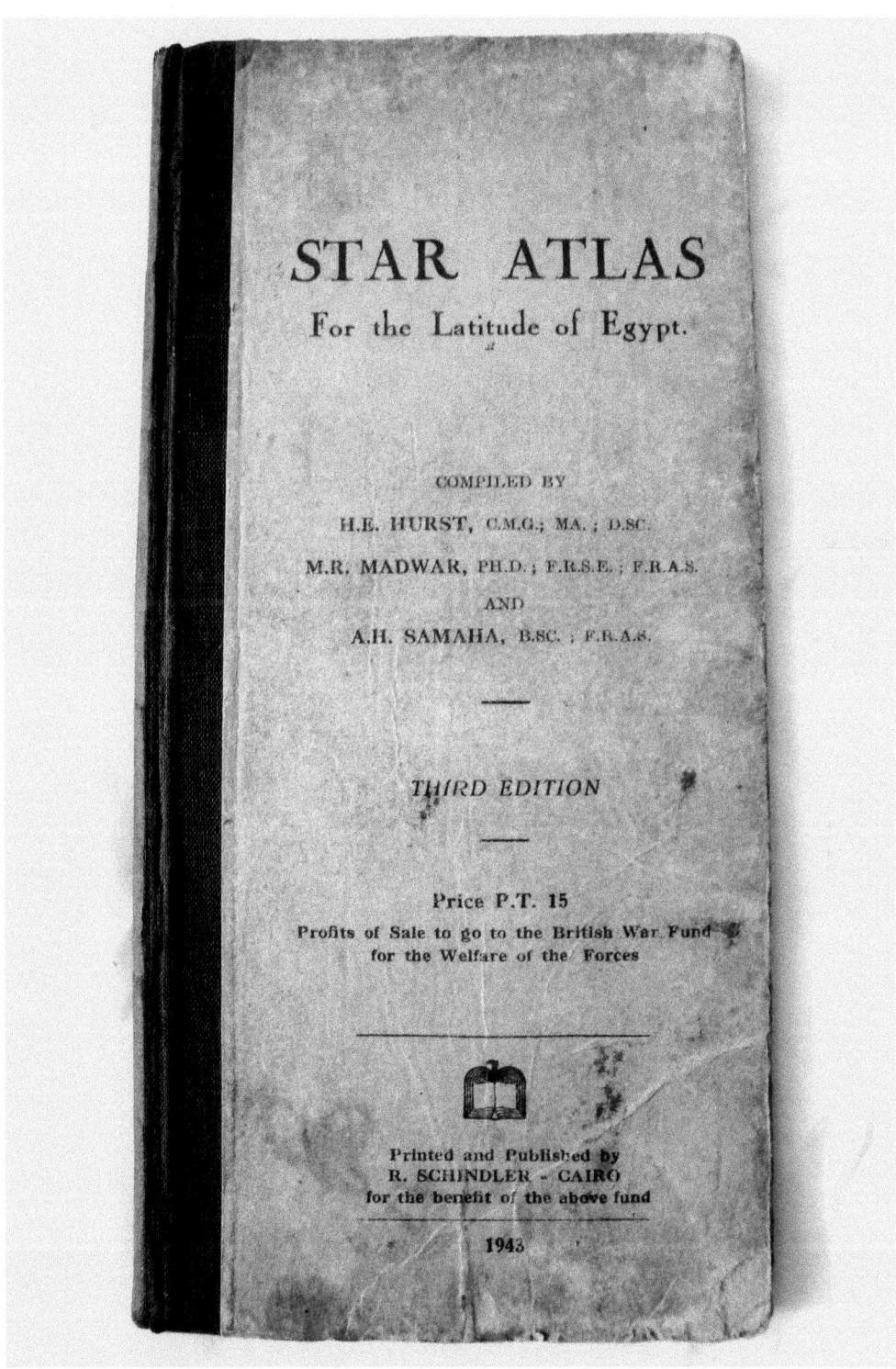

Star Atlas reference used to establish a position.

The Bagnold sun compass, the key LRDG daytime navigation tool. Using the shadow cast by the sun on the compass rose, it indicated the bearing on which the vehicle was travelling.

Azimuth Cards (Summer and Winter) for use with Bagnold sun compass.

Position being checked by R Patrol navigator Gunner C.O. 'Bluey' Grimsey (right) employing the sun compass. Man on left: unidentified.

(**Left**) *Hints on Map Reading Instruction* military manual, 1943. This example belonged to Captain C.K. Saxton, T Patrol LRDG. (**Right**) *Field Navigation, Dead Reckoning* wartime military manual, 1942.

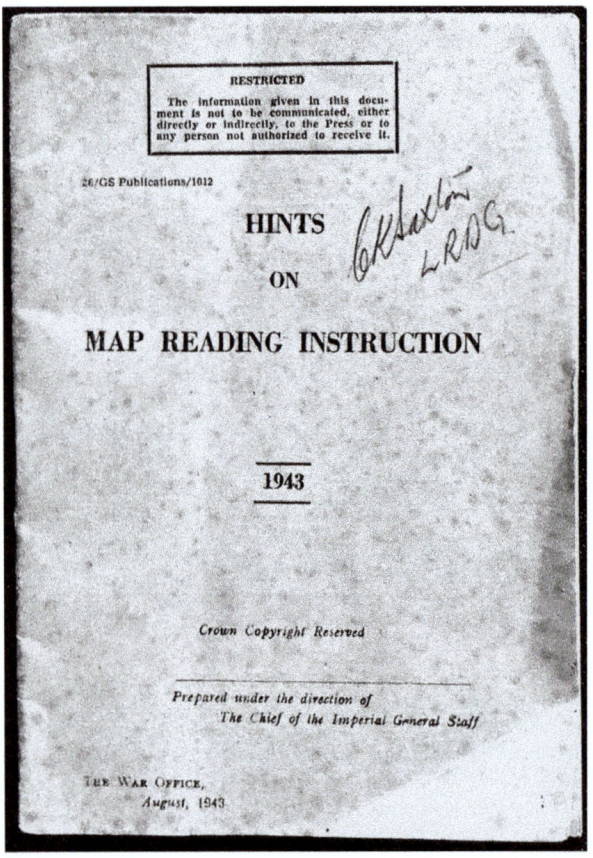
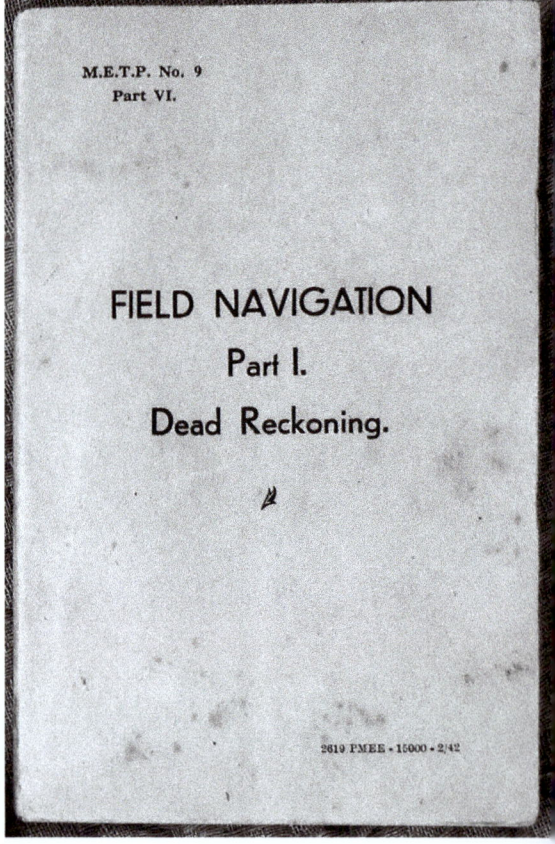

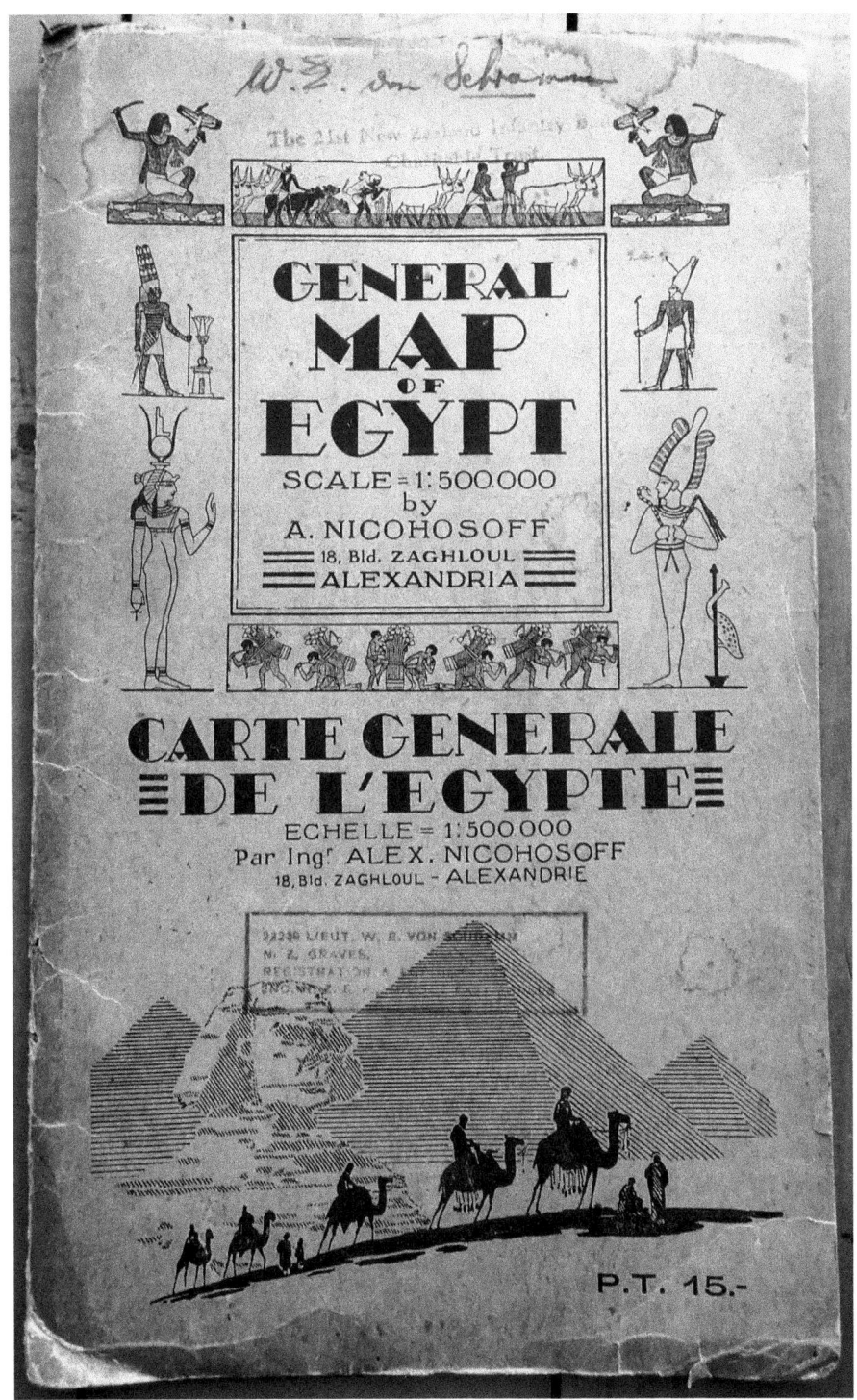

Wartime commercial map of Egypt adopted by the NZ Army as a reference map. Initially the LRDG had to employ Italian maps for information on the Libyan interior, but they proved unreliable.

(**Above**) T Patrol members halt to examine their map board. Left: Trooper I.G. McCulloch, Lieutenant S.W. Ellingham and Corporal G.C. Garven.

(**Opposite, above**) Topographical reconnaissance mapping missions were undertaken to create 'going' maps of areas for possible future operations. Y Patrol truck Y3 crosses rocky terrain as they try to negotiate a trail.

(**Opposite, below**) Y Patrol crossing a flooded wadi, an example of one of the difficulties the patrols encountered on their journeys, especially in the winter. Sand trays sometimes had to be used to help cross the boggy ground.

Captain N.P. Wilder (second left) reads a map as he confers with members of his T1 Patrol. They were undertaking a topographical charting mission to find a passable route into Tunisia.

Navigation training using a Bagnold sun compass in the foreground and a Coles compass on the bonnet. The vehicle is a Bedford MWD.

```
No. 2
NAVIGATOR'S TRUCK.

STANDARD LOAD        4,433                                    lbs.
                                                              4,657
Additional Load                  Guns
One No.11 W/T Set       83       Twin .303 BROWNING     72
1 extra 6 volt Batt.    35       3000 Rds in Belts
1 PHILLIPS SET          24          & Boxes            296
Rod & Windam Aerial )            Twin VICKERS "K"       62
Ops. Kit             )  25       16 Magazines           93
1 Theodolite            28       3000 Rds.             200
1 Map Press             10       2 Boxes Grenades       83
1 Navigator's Gear       5       Extra Cover & Tube    136
1 Aero Compass          12
                     ------                          ------
                      4,657                           5,578
```

A copy of an original document outlining equipment and supplies carried in the Chevrolet 1533X2 navigator's truck, 1942.

Lance Corporal R.C. (Ron) Davies wearing the LRDG issue *keffiyeh*. He and another were wounded when their camp at Ksar Rhilane was strafed by enemy aircraft. The patrol was undertaking a topographical mapping mission in Tunisia.

A very poor quality but rare photo of T2 LRDG men with US soldiers at Tebessa, Algeria, 1943. The patrol, while working with the PPA, had been shot up at Ksar Rhilane in Tunisia, and the men had to trek or if wounded be driven out for rescue. They sought assistance from the US First Army by crossing the border into Algeria to obtain transport to pick up the walking party.

Difficult going trying to negotiate the rolling sand dunes of the Grand Erg Oriental in Tunisia, 1943.

T2 Patrol members at Tebessa after seeking help from the US army after the patrol was shot up at Ksar Rhilane. Front left: Lance Corporal R.A. Ramsay, Corporal R.F. White, Trooper R.C. Davies, Trooper R. McBean, Private C.B. McKenzie, unidentified. Rear left: unidentified, Sergeant G.C. Garvin, unidentified, Trooper W.H. Burgess, unidentified, Private D. Munro, unidentified. Both Ramsay and Davies had been wounded.

A trooper observes the descent of the rest of his patrol coming over a ridge.

Chapter Six

Signals

For communication between each other and HQ, each patrol was equipped with the low-powered Army No. 11 wireless set. They had been used in tanks until the army replaced them with the No. 19 set. The No. 11 had proved very robust under all the conditions experienced. Breakdowns were uncommon and those that occurred were mostly after the sets had seen more than eighteen months' service. An example of its quality was when one set spent twenty-four hours under water in its vehicle in a flooded wadi. Taken from the truck and returned to HQ, it was found to be filled solid with mud. After cleaning it out, it worked and continued to function perfectly as it had before. Only on four occasions (other than enemy action) had a set broken down and left a patrol out of touch with HQ. Almost invariably the operators were able to fix a fault within a day or two. If signals totally failed due to enemy action or serious breakdown, the patrol usually returned home.

Power (12 volts) for the No. 11 set was obtained from the vehicle generator and battery with the addition of a further 6-volt battery and a 4-pole switch and an ammeter. Both batteries were switched in parallel across the vehicle generator for charging and in series across the set for working. This system had to be modified for use with Ford vehicles owing to the fact that the positive side of the vehicle battery was grounded to the chassis and the negative side of the set was of necessity also connected to the chassis. This meant the use of two extra batteries instead of one, and these were entirely divorced from the vehicle electrical circuit when working the set. Auxiliary charging equipment was only carried when it was anticipated that the patrol would be static for long periods. For example, on Road Watches charging sets could be used, which one operational report described as a 'Chorehorse Charging Engine', but these were noisy so some commanders preferred to take extra batteries instead.

The No. 11 had been designed for a range of only 15 kilometres, but when employed with Windom aerials that were slung between 5-metre poles, transmissions over great distances could be achieved. Care had to be taken to drop the masts as soon as aircraft were heard. When not in use the disassembled support poles were stowed strapped in sections at the top of the body side of the truck. For signals up to 800 kilometres a 1.8-metre rod aerial was adequate.

In addition, a Philips Type 635 receiver was carried for the GMT navigation time check, listening to music and the world news. The early Chevrolet WA trucks mounted their radio equipment in the body of the truck, whereas in all the later vehicles access was from the outside.

Each patrol included a radio truck which always travelled behind the commander's vehicle. It carried a fully qualified signaller while at least one other trained operator travelled in a different vehicle. In the LRP most of the operators were New Zealanders, but with the formation of the LRDG in November 1940, they were all drawn from the Royal Corps of Signals. The signaller's job was not an easy one and required great skill and concentration, especially after a long day's travelling when they often had to operate for two to three hours in the evening while most of the other patrol members were resting. On occasion the over-worked operator had to rest his hand for a while due to a condition known as 'telegraphist's cramp'.

A report was produced at the end of the desert war that presented an overview of the work of the LRDG Signals (WO 201/816 268890). Under the heading of 'Personnel', the following was explained:

> All signal personnel were handpicked volunteers. The patrol W/T operators were selected for intelligence, keenness and self-reliance rather than toughness, although they had to possess sufficient stamina to withstand the exposure of patrol life. Theirs was one of the hardest jobs of the patrol, demanding long hours of concentration when others were asleep or resting. Also a technical capacity above average in order to maintain their equipment for several weeks with no outside help and to site and operate a low-power W/T station over very great distances. To train an averagely competent B2 category operator for this job, approx. three weeks' intensive training at HQ followed by a month's work on an HQ control station were found necessary. A great many normally competent operators were found unsuitable and either used on Permanent Base Stations or returned to their units.
>
> The technicians at HQ were also hand-picked. The main task of the technical staff, in addition to maintenance of HQ signal equipment, was the inspection and preparation of patrol equipment. This required a high standard of training as the equipment was subject to very rough handling while on patrol and defects had to be anticipated rather than repaired. A breakdown on patrol probably necessitated the abandonment of an operation or affected its fulfilment to a marked degree.
>
> The provision of NCOs was always somewhat of a problem as it was the policy throughout the LRDG that no NCOs, except in a few isolated cases, were brought into the unit from outside. All had to revert on joining the LRDG and all promotions were made from within the unit. Yet patrol operators who were the most eligible to fill NCO vacancies were reluctant to accept promotion as it meant the cessation of patrol work for which they had originally volunteered.

Because security was vital in LRDG communications, all transmissions were passed in code. When in the field signals were destroyed every twelve hours, as were any working papers immediately after use. The Group as a whole used a system whereby frequencies were changed twice daily, with the call sign being altered at the same time. The patrols were expected to report to base at least once a day, usually in the evening or at meal times. After use the dials of the set were always tuned to zero in case the radio was captured and a frequency compromised. Air recognition signalling was the use of a sand mat painted with alternate red and white stripes, usually referred to in the reports as a 'Chequered Sand Mat'. This was laid out behind the vehicle if stationery or if moving along the centre of the load. In addition, formation signal flags were used as required to communicate between trucks.

Major D.G. Steele wrote in his recollections an extract about the importance of signals while on the Road Watch:

> I was in Siwa base HQ, expecting the usual evening report listing the day's Road Watch traffic tally when I got a yell from my radio operator to say that a cypher message was coming through from Marble Arch [the Road Watch area]. This was most unusual as the tally was always sent in a special code which was quicker to send than the cypher and meant that the patrol was not on the air too long. (An important thing, for the enemy was very quick with his RDF, and would soon have found where the watch was being kept.) Something must have gone wrong. It was a long message that seemed to take an age to come through, but at least we had it. Deciphered, it reported a new kind of enemy tank. The reference books did not list it and there were an awful number of them. The information was passed to Army in an 'Immediate' signal and we went in to have our dinner.
>
> When, after dinner, there was no reply from Army to my signal, I rang them on my scrambler and asked for the Senior Signals Officer. I told him about my message and asked why nothing was being done. (We could get away with anything, almost, in the LRDG.) He said he was sorry and would see to it personally. He would take it himself to the General.
>
> How we purred. There is nothing better for giving a lift to morale than telling a senior officer that his staff is slack and lazy and that they probably only reflect conditions in his office. It called for a drink at least. We had several as we sat back and waited. Then it came, the Chief of Staff Desforce himself on the phone. In future please make any similar signals 'Most Immediate'. Did we have any further details of the tanks? Aircraft would be sent out the next day to look for them near Benghazi. Could we arrange for the men who had seen the convoy to be picked up by plane and flown to Army HQ and so on. The aircraft were out next day and for several days, but found nothing. The men were delivered to HQ and made their report. Then all was quiet for some time, till the Hun threw in his new Mark IV tank into the battle up the coast.

A tragedy occurred on one patrol when a failure of signals led to an unfortunate friendly fire incident. On 20 February 1943, Lieutenant J.D. Henry, S2 Patrol, was operating with the Free French well behind their own lines when he saw what he took to be an Italian irregular camel patrol. A misunderstanding arose and shots were fired, during which Henry received a serious wound to his spine and his driver Private G.D. Rezin was killed. The 'enemy' was a party of Free French Méharistes, one of whom was also killed. They were from Tunisia, operating under orders from General Leclerc. The reason for the incident was attributed to the failure of Henry's radio which prevented Group HQ from warning him of the presence of these troops in his area. Henry died six months later as a result of his wound.

Chevrolet WA wireless truck *Rotowhero* cresting a sand dune. Note the aerial. The wireless-operator Signalman A. Pressick is behind a .55 Boys anti-tank rifle.

T Patrol members listen to the wireless that was housed within the Chevrolet WA truck.

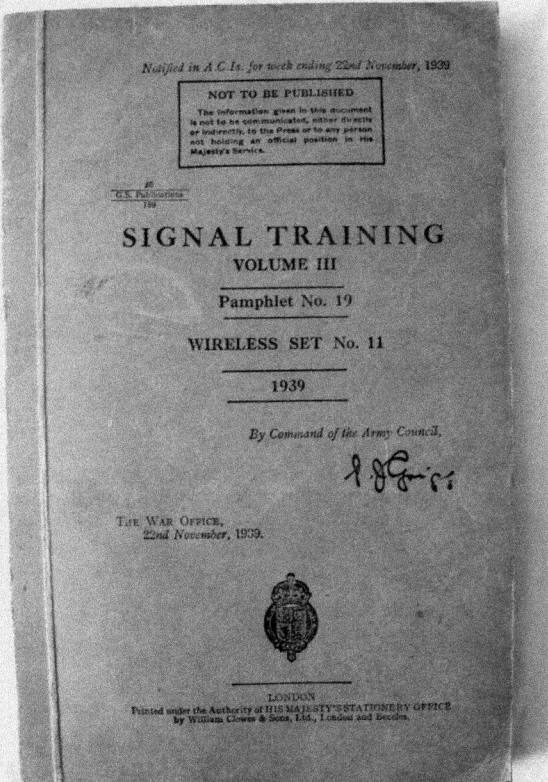

Military manual, *Signal Training Wireless Set No. 11*, 1939.

Plate III — WIRELESS SET No. 11 WITH SUPPLY UNIT L.P. No. 1 (IN CARRYING FRAME)

Labels: LEADS AERIAL No 1; CONDR. X5 5KV MK II; CARRIER No 1; AMMETER H.F. 350 m A. No 1; CONNECTOR 10 POINT No 1; LEADS EARTH No 2; SUPPLY UNIT L.P. No 1; LEADS EARTH No 5; LEADS EARTH No 1; CONNECTOR 3 POINT No 2; CONNECTOR 4 POINT No 2.

No. 11 wireless image taken from the *Wireless Set No. 11 Signal Training* manual.

Captured Italian SPA AS37 trucks were trialled by the LRDG. This example was fitted with a No. 11 wireless set.

General Claude Auchinleck alongside Captain L.B. Ballantyne examining a No. 11 wireless installed in the side of a Ford F30 truck. They were undertaking an LRDG inspection at the Abbassia barracks in Cairo.

Private G.D. Rezin, S Patrol, stands alongside his Ford F30 truck S4. He was later killed in action following a friendly fire incident. Their radio had failed, which meant the patrol was not aware of a Free French party in their area and shots were fired with fatal consequences on both sides.

(**Above**) A Y Patrol Ford F30 wireless truck. Note the fold-down side panel that serves as a table. The Phillips receiver is on the left next to the No. 11 wireless set. Right: Signalman K.L. Barbour next to Corporal A. Denniff. Left: Trooper A. Stacey (the other man is unidentified).

(**Opposite, above**) Signalman T. Scriven operates the No. 11 wireless enclosed in the side of a Chevrolet 1533X2. Note the Windom aerial pipe sections stowed above the radio housing. Next to the radio was a Phillips Type 635 receiver which was used for the GMT navigation time check and also to listen to the war news and music. The steel helmet is at the ready, usually worn if subject to aircraft bombing or strafing.

(**Opposite, below**) G Patrol men rest under a camouflaged wireless truck at Hatiet Etla, September 1942. Note the man sitting listening to the radio at the back right.

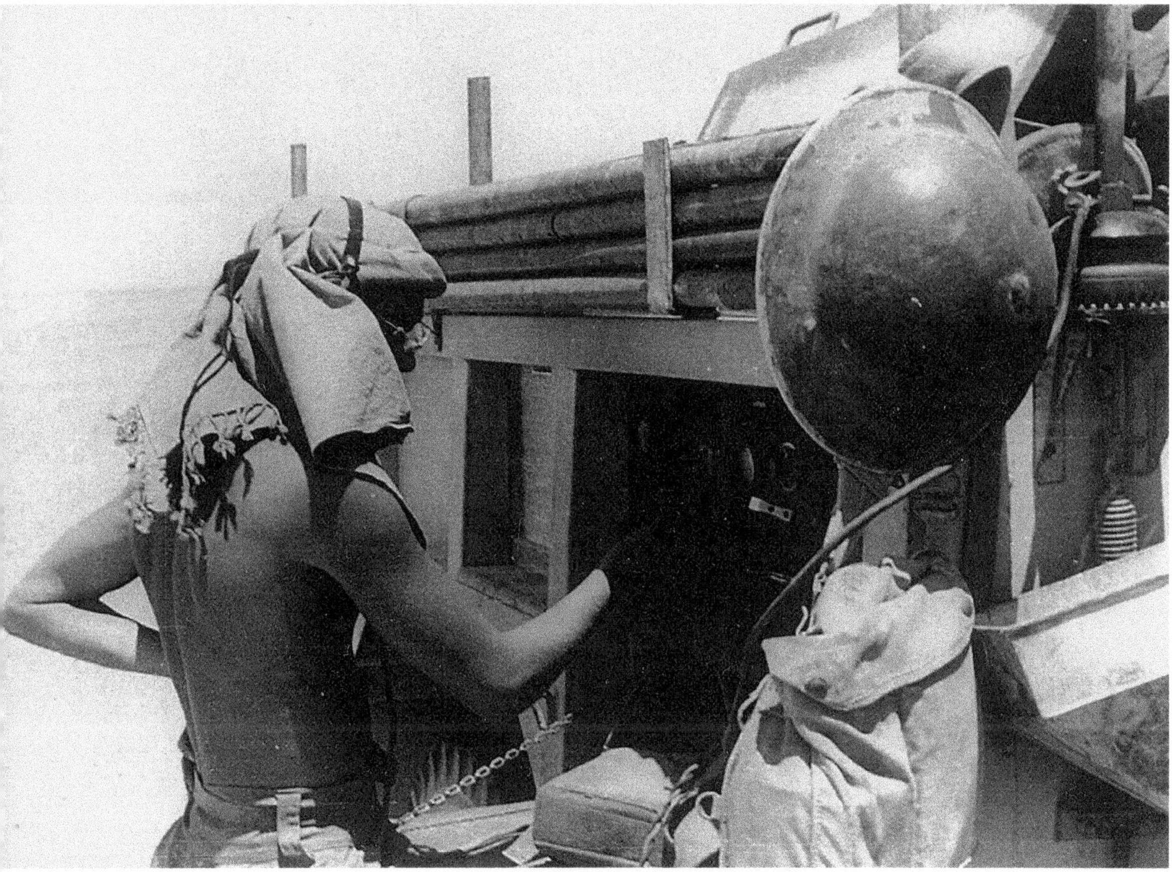

An S Patrol signaller wearing headphones next to his No.11 wireless set.

T Patrol members examining a Chorehorse charging engine that was used for recharging radio batteries. Left: Lieutenant R.H. Tinker talks to Corporal J.L.D. Davis.

Examples of original LRDG signal message forms.

T1 Patrol wireless truck *Te Aroha III*. The driver is Private T.E. Ritchie and alongside is Trooper F.W. Jopling. Top right is Signalman T. Scriven. The other men are unidentified.

A copy of an original document description of the various recognition signals when on patrol, 1943.

```
6.    COMMUNICATION.
      You will obtain Ciphers from S.O. L.R.D.G. and Signal instructions
from I.L.R.S. Sig Sergeant. You will report position and topographical
information when in your area, daily.

7.    RECOGNITION SIGNALS.
      Ground to Air.         Red & White chequered Sand Mats.
      British. Challenge  -  Blue flag waved anyhow.
               Answer     -  Blue flag held horizontally to left.
      French.  Sand Mats held horizontally.
               British    -  Red very light.
               French.    -  Green very light.
               British    -  Morse "B" with torch.
               French     -  Morse "V" with torch.
      American. Challenge -  Yellow flag waved anyhow.
                Answer    -  Yellow flag held horizontally, to left.
                             or Three green very lights.

DISTRIBUTION:-
    Captain A.B. Rand.  Copy No.  1.
    War Diary.            "   "   2-4.
    File.                 "   "   5.                    Major
    L.R.D.G.              "   "   6-9.     Comd Ind Long Range Squadron.
                                           AM
```

Sheet 14.

Long Range Desert Group
TRAINING NOTES.

8. FORMATION SIGNALS.

The following signals will be used in order to give control in the field. The signals can be given either by the arms or by flags but care must be taken that they can be clearly seen.

Every troop leader will carry on his vehicle the following flags:- green, black, yellow, and red. In addition the O.C. and 2 i/c. will each carry a white and blue signalling flag.

FLAG.	WHO ACTS.
Blue & White.	Used by the O.C. as an order to the patrol as a whole.
Green.	A (H.Q.) troop.
Black.	B Troop.
Yellow.	C Troop.
Red.	D Troop.

The following formation signals will be used either by the arms or by flag. The two flags used will normally be the blue and white flag, and the green flag, except where otherwise stated.

ORDER	SIGNAL	REMARKS
Prepare to advance.	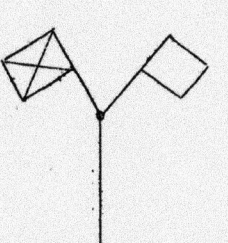	Drivers engage gears and prepare to move off.
Advance	Flags or arms dropped	Cars move off.
Halt.	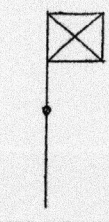	

A copy of the LRDG formation signal flags as described in *The Long Range Desert Group Training Notes,* January 1941.

Chapter Seven

Supplies

To maintain their long-range patrols the trucks carried almost 2 tonnes of stores. This initially included petrol in 4-gallon (18-litre) 'flimsy' tins, packed two to a wooden box, although due to the constant movement of the truck there was always a risk of leakage within the metal tins. On one S Patrol trip led by Lieutenant J. Henry on 4 November 1942, he recorded that out of thirty-four cases carried, 20 per cent of the flimsies had leaked fuel. Fortunately on that trip they were also carrying jerrycans, with forty-five per truck, none of which leaked. They became the preferred way of transporting fuel and water. The trucks were also stowed with tarpaulins, camouflage netting, bedrolls, spare wheels, tyres and springs, and munitions including land mines, water, cases of rations and rum jars.

From their earliest activities, the LRDG was placed on a special scale of rationing, distinct from that provided for troops of the Eighth Army and on base installations. It was presumed that patrols away on a trip did not always have the time or opportunity to cook in the field and quality rations had to be arranged accordingly. A balanced diet was essential for men engaged in such exhausting work.

The quartermastering branch of the LRDG seldom if ever dealt directly with the base ordnance depots because this method of obtaining supplies usually involved too much delay. As the Group's requirements had to be met almost immediately, it was placed on a very high priority by GHQ MEF. The units' demands were made directly to GHQ.

Veteran Merlyn Craw of T Patrol recalled the rations, which he described as generally better than that of the regular army:

> Mostly canned food, such as tinned bacon, M.V. stew, curried sausages, salmon, herrings, bully beef, baked beans, peas, cauliflower and Brussels sprouts. Also dried food like powdered potatoes, oatmeal, rice, spaghetti, tasteless egg powder and hard biscuit, plus Cyprus potatoes carried in a sack. Sometimes after a rough journey on a hot day the cans would hiss and 'wough!' when opened and the contents could occasionally look like cat food! The main meal was at night and everything went in the same pot. Dessert was tinned fruit, which was sweet and refreshing, followed by the evening rum issue, usually put in the tea. There was no fresh milk, apart from occasionally condensed milk which I was fond of. Some saved their rum to have a booze-up later. Fresh meat was usually only when we shot

and pot-roasted a gazelle. But you couldn't afford to be in a hurry, as these could be tough sometimes and took a long time to cook. Patrol members had to take turns to cook, though it was generally an unpopular duty and some of the men were lousy cooks.

The LRDG Waco aircraft would drop off bread and mail if the patrol was not raiding deep into the desert.

For cooking we dug a hole in the sand, poured petrol in and wood from the flimsy box. A 4-gallon tin was put on top, with the stew put in and the fire lit. Benghazi burners were used to boil the water for tea. When dinner was over, all tins, waste and benzine tins were squashed and buried so as not to give away our presence. The cups, plates, utensils and pots were cleaned with dry sand.

On one occasion in January 1942, while out from Siwa on another job, we had to travel via Giarabub to pick up petrol in drums. As for a time there was no cased petrol left in the Middle East, which was rather a pity, because although it was awkward stuff to handle in 4-gallon tins, two to each case, the wood of the box was very handy to start cooking fires with.

In 1981, LRDG veteran Bill Johnson wrote an article for the *LRDG Association Newsletter* where he described gazelle as a nice addition to the normal field ration:

We were sick of bully and biscuits so we used to shoot gazelle and eat them. The drill was to shoot only stags as the does might be in kindle and the meat tainted. The first time I saw it done I thought I'd never eat that, but I learnt to love it. First shoot a stag, drop the tailboard of the truck and with a sharp machete chop up the stag into joints. Dig a shallow slit trench, soak the sand with petrol, place over a well-polished sand tray and set fire to the petrol. Put the joints on the sand tray and the blue flames would come through the holes. Baste the joints with 10lb tins of butter. Bury all the innards and the skin.

But I never buried the skin. I kept them all in my truck and all the men in my patrol used to play merry hell with me as they attracted thousands of flies until I had dried them all off. Some months later we had a week's leave in Cairo. We parked up the trucks in Abbassia Barracks so I said to my driver, 'Get in, we are going to get rid of those gazelle skins!'

We found the handbag factory and I finished up, after a lot of bartering, getting 150 pounds sterling which we divided amongst the patrol.

Major D.G. Steele wrote his observations on rationing and the value of the rum issue:

The one thing above all else that made us the envy of the ME Forces was our ration scale. For this we have to thank the efforts of Lieutenant F.B. Edmundson, our Medical Officer. He was given the task of working out a scale of rations suitable for the proposed operations. Told to make up a ration which would keep the men fit and well over a long period with no fresh food, gruelling conditions of heat and water shortage along with the risk of boredom; he did a great job. Though I think I did once hear someone say, 'What, pineapple again!'

One of the greatest items in the issue was the rum ration. Time and time again this proved its worth. At the end of a long day pushing and hauling, unloading and carrying equipment to get trucks through soft sand, it was found that the men could not eat. However, after a tot of rum, they were new men in no time. Ready for their food and willing and able to do the numerous maintenance jobs necessary in the patrol. Bagnold on his prewar desert trips had found the tonic effect of rum. He demanded it for the LRDG and we got it, though it was not on general issue to the army.

Captain D. Barrett, Quartermaster LRDG, wrote in a report dated 3 May 1943 of the supply issues:

> Not infrequently the LRDG had to supply commando troops and other parties that might be attached to the Group for operational purposes. Not only did these people arrive without petrol and food, but very often they lacked essential equipment. It would appear that they regarded the LRDG as a sort of Royal Army Service Corps base supply depot, which was certainly not the case. This attitude sometimes caused embarrassment and difficulties in both camps. In addition, patrols occasionally picked up the crews of crashed aircraft, as well as escaped prisoners of war and stragglers, who had to be fed, clothed and provided with accommodation. There were few of these, however, and providing for them was not a matter of great concern.

Filling flimsy tins with water from the underground spring at Ain Dalla.

R Patrol men pumping ground water at Tazerbo.

Benzine boxes awaiting storage on the Ford F30 truck. Trooper I.G. McCulloch sits in the back.

SRD (Supply Reserve Depot) 1-gallon rum jars. They were packed two to a box to help prevent breakage. Bagnold on his pre-war desert trips had noticed the tonic effect of rum. He demanded it for the LRDG as a 'pick-me-up' after a long day of desert travelling or action. It was not on general issue to the regular forces.

A Ford F30 roughly packed with baggage and stores, including camouflage nets and bedding. Corporal R.O. Spotswood of R Patrol dressed for the cold.

The wood from the benzine boxes was used as fuel for the cooking fire. Left: Lance Corporal C.G. Ball, Trooper A.M. Saunders and Private R.H. Tinker.

R Patrol men enjoying a meal break. The dropped-down rear truck tray makes a useful dinner table.

Trooper M.E. Hammond of R Patrol poses at Siwa with a display of rations including gin. The LRDG enjoyed a good diet that kept them reasonably fit and healthy for the rigours of desert operations.

An S Patrol trooper enjoying a meal in the shade of his truck. A benzine case and flimsy tin made useful dining furniture.

Supplies being sorted at Kufra.

An R Patrol truck at Siwa. The 20-litre jerrycans were ideal for close packing and replaced the bulky flimsy tins packed in the wooden boxes. R10 was a fitter's truck; note the spare springs tied to the side.

Men posing against the Waco AX697 LRDG liaison aircraft. The LRDG had two Waco aircraft. These were used wherever possible to transport personnel including sick and wounded, and to carry urgent vehicle spares, mail and supplies.

Loading stores in preparation for a trip on T Patrol truck *Te Paki* T5. Private C.A. Dornbush places the boxes in the back.

The trucks were tightly packed with a variety of stores. Depending on the expected duration of a trip, the stores were carefully calculated on what was to be issued per man per day. Packed in the foreground is a metal 'camel' water tank.

Lieutenant A.R. Cramond, T2 Patrol, sitting in his tent at a semi-permanent desert base.

Rhodesian S Patrol men pose with a gazelle that they are about to prepare for dinner. This animal was a good source of fresh meat for the patrols.

After a long day on patrol, the serving of the evening meal was always very welcome.

(12)

L.R.D.G. MEDICAL KIT FOR PATROLS

The amounts of drugs and dressings issued vary with the time of the year and the length of the journey ᵠ   Articles starred are only issued to R.A.M.C. Personnel when available.

```
1 Stretcher                   :  TABLETS.
1 Thomas Splint(complete)     :  Aspirin  )              50
3 strips of Cramer            :  Dovers   ) Pain Killers 12
        Splinting.               Morphine )  gr ¼        30
Extra Water Bottles.          :
------------------------         Morphine gr¼ in glass
                                    tubes (20 Tabs)      1
Bandages-assorted 2-3 doz.  :                         Tube
Slings                  4
Elastoplast - roll      1     :  Morphine in phials
Zinc Plaster Roll       1           for injection ᵠ     10
Many tail Abdominal           :                       phials
        Binder          1        No.4 Cough              50
Cotton Wool             4 oz. :  No.8 Diarrhoea          50
Gauze                   6 pkts   No.9 Constipation       12
Lint - small roll       1     :  Bismuth Indigestion     30
Jaconet                 1 Sq.Ft. Quinine  fever         100
Shell Dressings         6     :  Lysolats disinfectant.  1
------------------------                               Box
                              :  Acroflavine Antiseptic
Eye Bath                            Lotion for wounds   1
Spencer Wells Forceps                                Bottle
Scissors                      :
Tourniquet                       Pot. Permang. Mouth or
Safety Pins                   :      Foot wash.
Water Sterilizing Powder
Needles ᵠ                     :  Sulphonamide - wounds   40
Syringe 2 cc for                 M & B 693  Bad chests
        Morphia.                       G.C.,
                              :        Head wounds      25
                                 -----------------------
                              :  Ointments.
                                 Vaseline            1 tube
                              :  Desert sore (Sulphonamide)
Argyrol - Eye drops 1 oz.                            2 oz.
Boric Powder - Eye lotion :      Antiseptic  (H.A.D.) 2 oz.
        Feet 3 oz.               Healing (Zinc)       2 oz.
Tannifax - Burns    1 tube       Pile (Tannic Acid)   2 oz.
```

Copy of original document, the 'LRDG Medical Kit for Patrols', November 1942.

(5)

MAN WITH KIT (Winter)	lbs.	SPARE PARTS, CHEVROLET.	lbs.
Bed Roll	40	2 Radiators & Hose	85
Sheepskin Coat)		1 Distributor	7
or Greatcoat &)	12	1 Carburettor	6
Jerkin)		1 Generator	25
Helmet	3	1 Coil	3½
Mess Tin & Mug	2	1 Cut-out	3
2 Water-Bottles	7½	1 Starter Motor	17
Clothing	12	1 Fuel Pump & 2 Bowl Joints	3
Man	140	2 Fuel Pump Repair Outfits	1½
	248½	1 Water Pump & Repair kit	8
		1 Fan	4
		6 Fan-Belts	2¼
		2 Valves, inlet) Assemblies	
		2 " Exhaust)	3½
		2 Push Rods	½
TRUCK EQUIPMENT		2 Tappetts	½
	lbs.	1 Con rod	4
2 Sand Mats	34	1 Piston & Rings	3¼
2 " Trays	74	1 Rubber Engine Mounting	½
Tarpaulin & Camouflage	122	1 Thrust Race	½
2 Spare wheels	380	2 Clutch Plates	10
Standard Kit, Jack, Spanners etc.	80	1 Universal Joint & Four bearings	2
2 Gallon Oil Tin	22	1 Steering Column & Box & Drop Arm	20
Tow Chain	50	1 Half Shaft	21
Spade	4	1 Track Rod (or ends)	5
Matchett	2	1 Rear Spring & Main Leaf	106
Torch Hand	1	1 Front " " " "	52
	769		

Copy of original document indicating the weight in pounds of supplies and equipment to ascertain truck-loading capacity.

(11)

L.R.D.G. Ration Scale.

G.O.,42 of March   CRLME/444/Q.

1. Bacon tinned..........2½ ozs.	Sugar..........3½ ozs
2. Bread................16 "	Tea...............¾ "
3. Biscuits.............12 "	Vegs.tinned....4 "
3. Cheese...............1½ "	Ascorbic tabs + 1 Tab.
4. Chocolate............2 "	Marmite ǫ ......3/28 oz.
5. Curry Powder........1/8 "	Rum ₽ ....1 "
6. Fruit dried.........4/7 "	or Cocoa........1 pint.
7. Fruit tinned.........4 "	or Tea..........1 " "
8. Herrings............1¼ "	Tobacco or
9. Jam, M/Lade or Golden	Cigarettes......2 ozs
Syrup..1½ "	per week.
10 Lime Juice.........1/16(Bott)	Matches.........2 boxes
11 Margarine...........1½ ozs.	per week.
12 Meat Preserved......6 "	
with pickles........1 "	
chutney..........¼ "	+ To be issued in special
13 Meat Loaf or Ham and	circumstances only at
Tongue..1¼ "	the discretion of the
14 M & V...............2 "	Patrol Commander.
15 Milk tinned.........2 "	
16 Mustard............1/100"	ǫ To be issued only under
17 Oatmeal or Flour....2 "	the authority of a
18 Onions..............2 "	Divisional or equivalent
19. Pepper............1/100"	Commander.
20 Potatoes tinned.....3 "	
21 Salt...............¾ "	Total daily weight
22 Salmon tinned.......1 "	(less containers - 4lbs 2oz.
23 Sardines............1 "	With containers say 5lbs
24 Sausages............1 "	

Copy of original document of LRDG Ration Scale, March 1942.

Chapter Eight

Weapons

The first patrols carried .303 Lewis guns, .303 Vickers heavy machine guns, .55 Boys anti-tank rifles and one truck-mounted 37mm Bofors anti-tank gun, plus personal weapons, namely the .303 Lee Enfield service rifle, .45 Thompson sub-machine guns and Webley or Enfield .38 revolvers. Furthermore, 2in mortars and .303 SMLE EY grenade-launching rifles were carried and employed with some success. In the beginning, the patrol's primary task was reconnaissance, with armaments generally being carried for self-defence or for use in small-scale attacks against supply convoys and lightly-defended Italian emplacements.

However, over time, the patrols took on a more aggressive role and the weaponry increased. With the replacement of the Ford F30s by the 1942 Chevrolets, they progressed to mounting heavier armament with greater fire-power, which increased their offensive capability. Initially they continued with the .303 Lewis and water-cooled Vickers, and then used whatever they could find from crashed aircraft or wrecked vehicles; for example, adopting tank Besa machine guns, and also employing single or twin .303 Aircraft Pattern Browning machine guns fitted with mountings made in the LRDG workshops. The operational consideration was setting the correct aiming distance. The twin-mounted guns were arranged fighter-style with the brace of guns fitted to fire not at a parallel trajectory but slightly toed inwards to create a fixed point where the bullets would strike at a single point over a certain distance.

Some weapons were taken from the enemy, such as Italian Breda 12.7 machine guns. The Boys .55 anti-tank rifles, carried since the beginning, were now removed as they were of little use. Armoured vehicles were rarely encountered by the LRDG, and if so, were avoided as quickly as possible.

After a time the Lewis guns were replaced with the .303 Vickers K. These were fed by a 100-round flat pan magazine and proved very effective, especially when mounted as a dual combination. Originally designed as RAF air gunners' weapons, they were favoured by both the LRDG and SAS for their reliability and firepower. Heavier-calibre weapons were now also being acquired. Initially, in February 1942, seventeen water-cooled .5in Vickers Mk IV heavy machine guns were supplied. These were later replaced by the lighter air-cooled .50 Brownings, both Air Pattern and HB models which became the standard and were often mounted on the jeeps.

With the new Chevrolets, the cumbersome heavy single-shot Bofors gun was discarded and replaced by the more versatile Italian semi-automatic 20mm Breda Model 35 gun. This was mounted on a carriage turntable, bolted through the rear deck onto the truck chassis. Operated by a crew of two, they fired a twelve-round clip and proved to be a very effective and dependable weapon. One was attached to each patrol. By 1942/43, the truck-mounted weapons could prove very devastating against concentrated enemy targets such as road convoy attacks or on enemy airfields as in the Barce raid.

Using 'hit-and-run' tactics they would ambush Axis road convoys, roadhouses, supply dumps, airfields, attack any targets of opportunity and then would melt away into the desert. They referred to these actions as 'beat-ups'. The LRDG came and went so quickly that the Italians called them *Pattuglia Fantasma* (Ghost Patrols) because they never knew where or when these raiders were going to strike next. This caused the Axis forces so much concern that they were forced to withdraw badly-needed troops, armour and aircraft from the front lines to protect their rear areas. Part of their success lay in being such a small force that could easily conceal themselves behind enemy lines in the shadows of dunes and wadis, or widely disperse to become difficult to find.

The LRDG required large stocks of ammunition and different types of explosives for a 'road beat-up' or a raid, such as those at Barce or Sirte. A patrol would expend about 40,000 rounds of small-arms ammunition and at any time a great deal would be blazed away at aircraft that frequently attacked the patrols in the course of an operational trip or reconnaissance. The RAF assisted the LRDG by supplying Vickers K and Browning machine guns and specially-belted ammunition. There were also a number of air-raids on Kufra, Siwa and Jalo, which were visited by reconnaissance aircraft. The enemy dropped a few bombs. The chief target at Siwa was an unserviceable RAF ambulance plane, the only machine visible there.

(**Opposite, above**) LRDG men with the .303 Lewis gun placed in an anti-aircraft position. The loader has a spare forty-seven-round pan magazine at the ready. The gun was widely used in the LRDG right through to late 1942 when more effective weapons became available. The exposed magazine could sometimes be a disadvantage in the dust-blown desert, causing it to jam.

(**Opposite, below**) A Vickers .303 water-cooled heavy machine gun. In the background General Claude Auchinleck inspects the LRDG at Abbassia, Cairo, 1941. Stowed below the gun is a .303 Lee Enfield Mk III service rifle. These were usually carried on all the trucks.

Vickers machine-gun practice in the desert. Trooper R.C. Davies is behind the weapon.

A size comparison between the .50 Vickers Mk V (top) and the .303 Vickers.

A grenade-discharger cup fitted to the end of a reinforced EY .303 Lee Enfield rifle. Also shown is a tin of seven-second fuses with the grenades that were launched by these weapons.

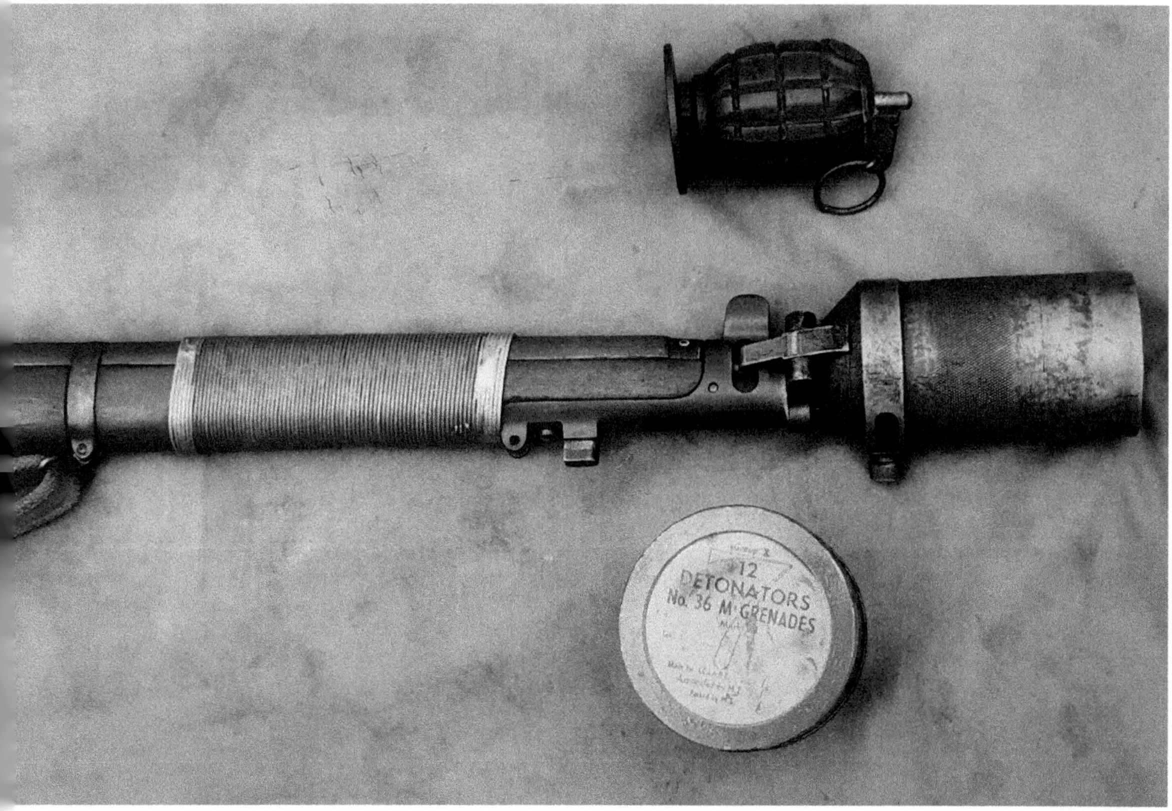

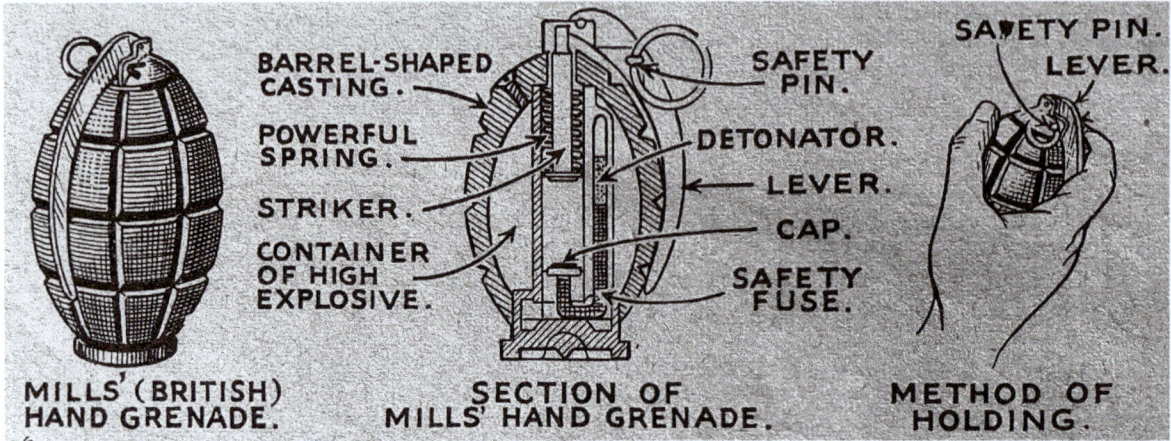

An illustration of the British No. 36M hand grenades from the wartime magazine *The War Weekly*. These were carried in the trucks and used in close action encounters like road convoy attacks or raids such as on Barce town and airfield.

A .45 Thompson M1928 A1 submachine gun displayed against an LRDG canvas kitbag; a much-favoured LRDG and SAS weapon. The LRDG mostly operated them with the straight twenty-round magazine. Also shown was the heavier and less-employed fifty-round drum magazine.

COPY

SECRET

Subject : Controlled Stores for LRDG.

CRME/4573/1/GSD2a.

OS3
---

1. The release of the following controlled stores for 'S' and 'T' patrols, LRDG is approved :-

    TSMG's   2
    Spectacles Tinted   100
    Binoculars H.P.   4
    Compasses Liquid   4
    Mortars 2"   2
    LMG's Lewis .303"   4
    Rifles E.Y.   2
    Pistols   1
    Rifles no.1 Mk III 10
    Pistols Signal   1

2. Might the above receive immediate attention as the unit is demanding forthwith on 4 BOD.

(Sd) C H Finlay

Lt-Col,
G.S.

Ext:340
GSD.2a.
20 Jan 42.

FCM

An LRDG 'Controlled Stores' list that includes weapon requirements for S and T Patrols, dated 20 January 1942.

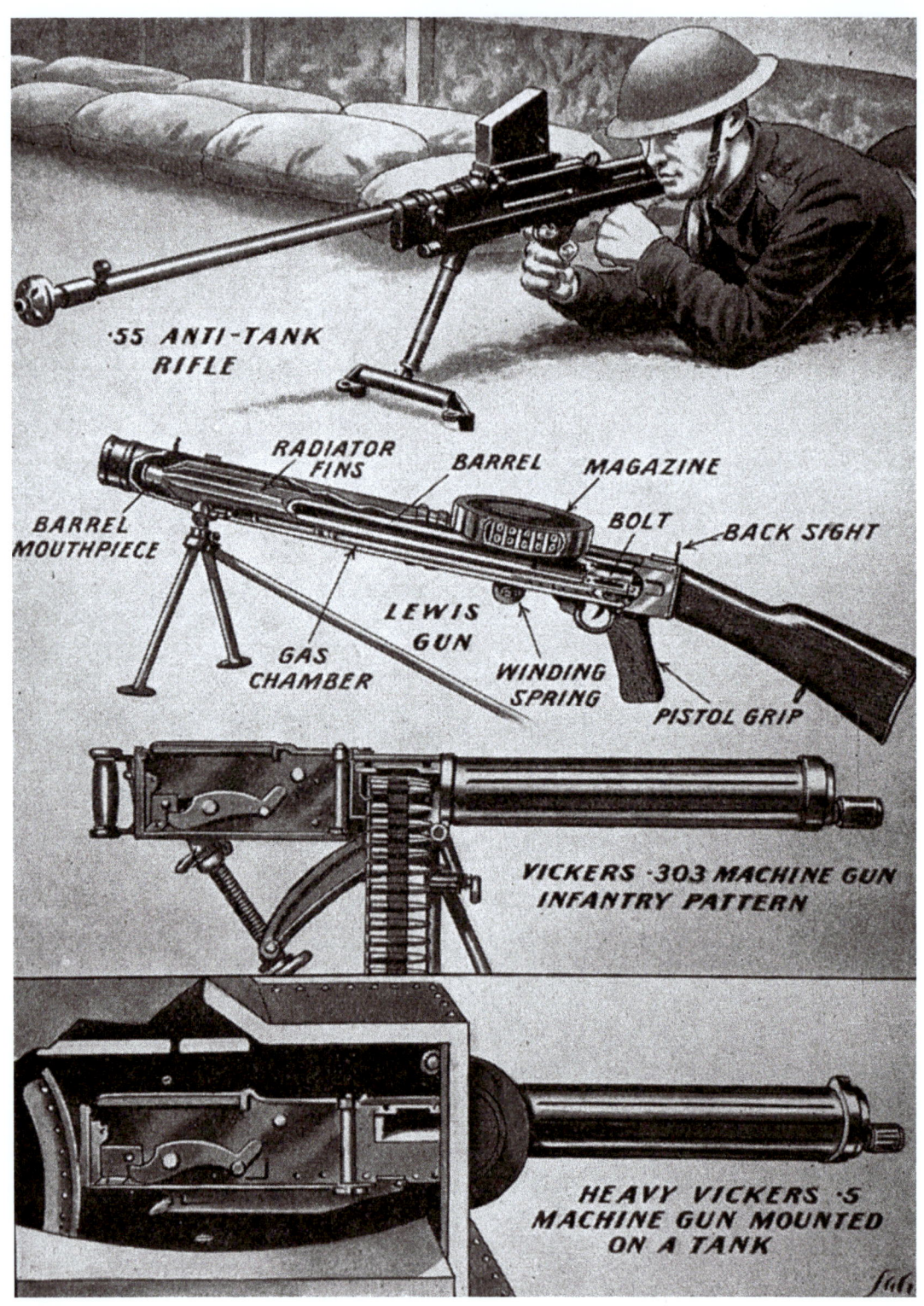

```
SUBJECT:                    Ammunition.

                                              Group H.Q.,
                                              L.R.D.G.
                                              -----------
                                              14th November, 1942.
                                              ----------------------
To:-       O.C., "A" Squadron  (5 copies)
           O.C., "B"    "      (7   "   )
           I.O.
           Q.M.
           ----------------------------------------

           The only scale of Ammo authorised for
Patrols is set out below:-

     .303 Automatic M.G.s       1500 Tracer       1500 rds.
          (Except BROWNING)      450 Incend.
                                 000 Ball
     .303 BROWNING                                1500
     .45  T.S.M.G.                                 250
     9 mm STEN                                     250
     .5 M.G.                                      1000
     12.7 mm BREDA                                 500
     20 mm BREDA                                   500
     Grenades 4 sa                                   6 boxes
        "    7 sa                                    4   "
        "    68 (Anti-tank)                          1   "

           Patrols holding ammunition surplus to the
above scale will return same to the Q.M. forthwith.

           Any Patrol holding ammunition below this
scale will draw up their deficiencies from the Q.M.

                                              Captain,
                                         Adjutant, L.R.D.G.
Field.
A.B.
```

(**Above**) An ammunition supply list indicating the variety of munitions used by the patrols, dated 14 November 1942.

(**Opposite**) A wartime illustration from *The War Weekly* magazine showing the weapons employed by the LRDG at different times during the desert war. The heavy water-cooled .5in Vickers Mk IV was originally mounted in light tanks. Seventeen were adopted by the patrols and mounted on their trucks. These created significant additional firepower and were later replaced by the lighter air-cooled .50 calibre Brownings, both Air Pattern and HB models.

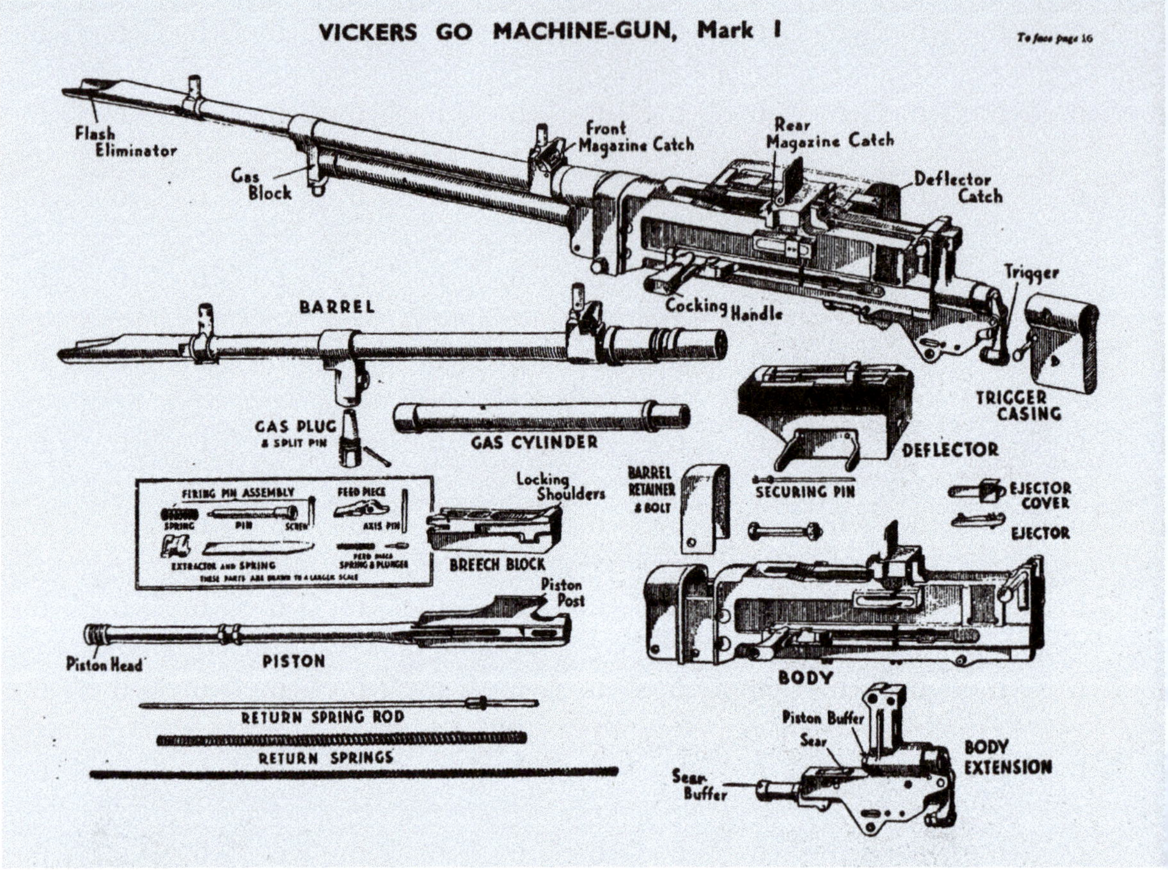

A diagram of the components of the .303 Vickers K (GO, gas-operated) machine gun. As illustrated in the July 1943 *Military Training Manual No. 35, Vickers GO Machine Gun Mark I*.

Trooper K. Tinckler sits behind the wheel of the Y Patrol wireless truck mounting twin Vickers K machine guns. The guns with their 100-round flat pan magazines produced a high volume of fire.

Captain N.P. Wilder targets a .303 Vickers K machine gun. The holster on the side contained a Verey flare pistol for signalling.

A Vickers K mounted on the passenger's side of the truck. This one is unusual as it has been fitted with Vickers heavy machine gun wooden grips. Left: Private C.A. Dornbush and Trooper A.G. Ferguson undertake engine maintenance.

A .37 Bofors anti-tank gun mounted in the rear of a Chevrolet WA truck. Gunner E. Sanders is on the right.

A Ford F30 Bofors gun truck, Y Patrol, Y7.

An unusual aerial view of the Bofors gun mount fixed in the rear of a Ford F30. The driver is Trooper J.P.L. Macassey, T Patrol.

T2 Patrol Chevrolet Breda truck, T10. An Air Pattern .303 Browning is mounted on the passenger's side. The driver is Private C.B. McKenzie.

Private C.B. McKenzie sitting behind a 20mm Breda Model 35 gun mounted in the rear of a Chevrolet.

A close-up of the pair of .303 Browning Air Pattern machine guns. Using recovered guns from downed RAF aircraft, the mountings and firing mechanisms were usually fitted in the LRDG workshops. Note the Kiwi painted on the bumper indicating it is a T Patrol truck. Left, Lieutenant R.A. Tinker.

A soldier poses alongside an abandoned 20mm Breda Model 35 gun. They were a very effective and dependable semi automatic weapon that was fed by 12 round clips. See clip on ground, bottom left. The LRDG adopted captured examples and mounted them in the rear of one Chevrolet 1533X2 in each patrol. These replaced the heavy single shot .37mm Bofors gun previously used.

T2 Patrol halted in the desert. Note the twin aircraft Brownings mounted on the F30 truck. The jeep mounts a single Vickers K.

Corporal M.H. Craw alongside his truck T5 *Te Paki III* prior to the Barce raid in September 1942. He is checking his .303 ammunition belts that will be used with the aircraft Brownings mounted on his truck. Note a broken rum jar on the ground.

Trooper R.C. Davies sits on a crash-landed RAF Kittyhawk fighter. The aircraft .303 Browning machine guns were sometimes recovered from downed aircraft and mounted on LRDG vehicles.

Chapter Nine

At Rest

The LRP was first based at Abbassia and the Citadel in Cairo. Then in early 1941, the LRDG began to expand into the desert regions. By the end of April, R, S and T Patrols were at Kufra and G and Y at Siwa. As their range of operations extended, all the patrols took turns in those bases and others were also set up as the war progressed at Tazerbo, Jalo, Fayoum, Zella and Hon.

These desert bases could be hot and uncomfortable, ridden with flies, snakes and scorpions and were on occasion subject to huge sandstorms. Kufra was the biggest oasis in Libya: it had an Italian-built fort and airfield occupied by the Free French and hundreds of palm trees surrounding a salt lake. The patrols could set up camp beside a well among the palm trees or in the native mud or stone huts. The Italians had built a pool with a windmill pump to store water, but it also made a good swimming pool. The heat was oppressive in the summer and made life difficult for the men, as Trooper R.W.N. (Dick) Lewis of T Patrol wrote in his diary:

> Sunday, 11 May 1941: Very hot again today. A lot of the chaps are feeling sick, some with gyppo guts and others just unable to keep their food down. Our skin abrasions soon turn into desert sores that gradually get bigger and deeper and hurt quite a lot. Kufra is as hot as anywhere in the Sahara, with grown-up men having never seen the rain.
>
> When the Khamseen blew at Kufra it was like gusts of hot air from an open stove, with squalls of wild driving sand and burning wind. Not bad when you are in a solid building, but living close to nature as we had to, it made you realize the hardiness of the desert dweller.

Lance Corporal E.M. (Mick) Allen, a British RAMC medical orderly attached to the LRDG wrote:

> While the LRDG was in the Kufra area, a shortage of medical supplies occurred. Sufficient quantities of all supplies had been provided in the first place, but liquids evaporated in the excessive heat. Other supplies, food and equipment deteriorated rapidly, until at one time we were right out of such essentials as iodine. This was a serious situation as we had no facilities at all for a while to treat urgent cases.

Lance Corporal Allen also described the conditions at Tazerbo:

> During my two years' service with the LRDG, the great majority of men enjoyed very good health. But during a summer at Tazerbo there was a

marked deterioration in the general standard of fitness. The heat at the time, 130 degrees in the shade, was so great that the men had to lie in the shade of their vehicles from 0800 to 1700 hrs daily. Although they were used to walking about barefooted, they could not stand the heat of the sand on their feet. At that stage malaria, dysentery and desert sores began to occur amongst the men.

Tazerbo is also the worst place we had ever known for flies. When the flies ceased to pester us at nightfall, we were at once attacked by mosquitoes. At daybreak, the man on piquet invariably found his back literally covered in flies. There was not room among them to place a pin. At meal times they used to drive the men practically crazy. In sheer desperation, I have also seen men sit over a fire with their faces in the smoke in order to eat their meals in comparative comfort.

Major D.G. Steele recorded his impressions of Siwa:

Life in the oasis of Siwa was fairly pleasant on the whole. We could buy a few fresh vegetables from the locals and at one stage oranges were in fair supply, also the odd egg. Siwa is noted for its dates, but the main attraction was the numerous springs. These varied in size from a few feet across to about ten yards. The larger ones like Cleopatra and the Figure Eight pools were enclosed with stone walls and fairly deep and made first-class swimming pools. The water was cool, clear and only very slightly saline. Here the troops spent most of their leisure time and inter-patrol water polo competitions were very popular. Near one of the pools we made tennis courts by rolling the salt mud with trucks and surrounding the area with camouflage netting.

For living quarters we had some native mud huts or houses, though some of the men preferred to sleep in the open where it was cooler. These mud houses of Siwa were rather interesting. They were built from the material available on site, a mixture of mud, salt and water. The salt is there from the evaporation of the more or less brackish spring water. When dry, the mixture sets like concrete and remains so unless there is heavy rain. Since there are only a few brief showers, as a rule, in the winter, this means the buildings are more or less permanent. In the old town, which has been partially demolished by the Egyptian Army for reasons of health and public safety, some of the ruins stood seven or eight storeys high. The roof beams were grown on the spot, being date palm trunks that were split in two and made happy hunting grounds for scorpions.

Gunner Grimsey, R Patrol, recorded in his diary his visit to the Free French fort at Zouar in January 1941. They had just completed an eleven-day journey over rugged landscape from Siwa:

We have arrived in a country of flora and fauna. To see green trees and birds and to find natural shade after the pitiless glare of the desert was to us something far from commonplace. Zouar is not an oasis and the water, what little there is, had to be drawn from deep wells. It has an earth taste. There are no palms, but many gum Arabic trees and large green bushes which somehow seem to provide sustenance for the goats and donkeys. Great sandstone hills that enclose this wide wadi stretch east and west and its surface is composed entirely of fine powdery sand from which the trees and bushes sprout.

The natives, Tibu, live mostly in the hills and the labour of the fort is done mostly by the natives the French have brought with them from around Lake Chad. Huge men with skin like polished ebony and of better physique than the small and sinewy Tibu. The Tibu used to make raids upon the Saras of the Lake Chad region and enslave them to sell to the Turks. These Tibu nomad tribes have been a venturesome enterprising people in their earlier history. They cover thousands of miles to make raids and drove their goats and livestock hundreds of miles to sell at other oases such as Kufra, in exchange for dates and grain which are not procurable in their own region.

16 January 1941: We find the French almost overwhelming with their hospitality. They have lost none of their reputation for preparing meals despite the difficulties presented by active service in the desert. The other night I dined under a gum Arabic tree and squatted on a goat skin spread on the sand while the meal was being prepared on a little wood fire built around stones. It was protected from the wind by an old mudguard from a derelict truck. First the soup was prepared; it was brought to the table, benzine boxes, by an obsequious Sara, as dignified as any English butler. Next came a drink of red wine, a cigarette and some parlez-vous punctuated by gesticulation and tracings in the sand. Then followed a course of beans and large juicy lumps of pork. Our plates were again removed and washed by the native servant. They were returned laden with little chunks of roasted meat, very tasty. The fourth course was rice, chopped meats and potato with olive oil. Our cups were kept filled with wine until the fifth course of tinned fruit was served. The sixth was sweet black coffee and biscuits. After this, the table was cleared and we settled down to some steady drinking and talking, which by this time proved entertaining for both parties. The whole meal took about two hours and I could not help comparing it with the manner in which we gobble down our stew of all number of things thrown in together. These French eat no breakfast, but dine about midday and at about eight o'clock in the evening. Wine and coffee are their chief drinks, while a spirit called tapia, which seemed to be rather like our whisky, was in much evidence.

30 January 1941: Been here a fortnight now, the flies are getting pretty bloody awful and I would hate this to develop into another Tazerbo. Fortunately, the days are only moderately warm and the nights cool. Meanwhile, in the camp Clarke Waetford [Trooper C. Waetford] with his hot sand oven has been cooking delicious dishes of roast goat and beef, while his brother Tom [Private E.B. Waetford] has worked for days on a Browning gun

retrieved from a plane. He has made a splendid job of the bolt and sights which we all thought far too complicated a job for any but an expert. He even made use of my theodolite to get the levels right. These two Maori boys put the rest of us to shame for energy and ingenuity. There seems no end to their confidence in carrying out what appear to be almost impossible tasks.

Major Steele also reflected on the welcome journey from their desert bases to Cairo for leave:

Cairo leave from time to time was a welcome change and provided some innocent fun on the run into town. The road from Matruh to Cairo was strewn with checkpoints manned by the British MPs who had a habit of detaining people who had no leave pass and movement orders. As we never issued either, there was at first a certain amount of hold-up until we hit on the idea of driving straight through or round the roadblocks. As we always travelled fast there were some exciting chases and when we finally stopped and asked the MPs what they wanted, they would nearly burst a boiler. We would then say, 'We are from the LRDG, you can report on us to whom you please, stand back, good day!' And we drove on. They did not like it, but Bagnold had always said there was too much red tape in the army, and we believed him. It worked at any rate and we never heard any more about it from the Provost. No doubt it was bad from the point of view of general army discipline, but it was good for patrol morale.

Corporal M.H. Craw of T Patrol recorded his memories of going on leave in Cairo:

The first thing was to have a shave, a bath and a cold beer, or go to a nice restaurant. But for some, the next thing was to visit the brothels. For myself and a few others we did not go to the brothels, but I can understand those who did, because after coming back from a patrol we knew we only had a week or so then we would go out again. So thinking perhaps for the last time, they used to drink heavily and go to those places. An amusing time, shortly after taking off on patrol again, some got itches after attending the blue light districts. The army used to dock the pay of any soldier who got VD, but if they went to the PA [prophylactic] Centre he was OK. I was not much of a drinker. I preferred an ice cream sundae when I was in Cairo. The military had advised that ice cream sold in Egypt may not be safe, but I never had a problem with it. To counter that, an ice cream factory was set up at Maadi camp for the soldiers to enjoy. General Freyberg also established a New Zealand Club in Cairo, where his off-duty soldiers could get a decent meal and a drink in a friendly environment. There was also a library, accommodation, bath and shower facilities.

Trooper A.H.C. Nutt overlooks the ancient town of Siwa in Egypt where the LRDG had established a base.

Major P.A. Clayton resting after a meal in the shade of his Ford 01 command car. He was later captured during the Fezzan operations in January 1941.

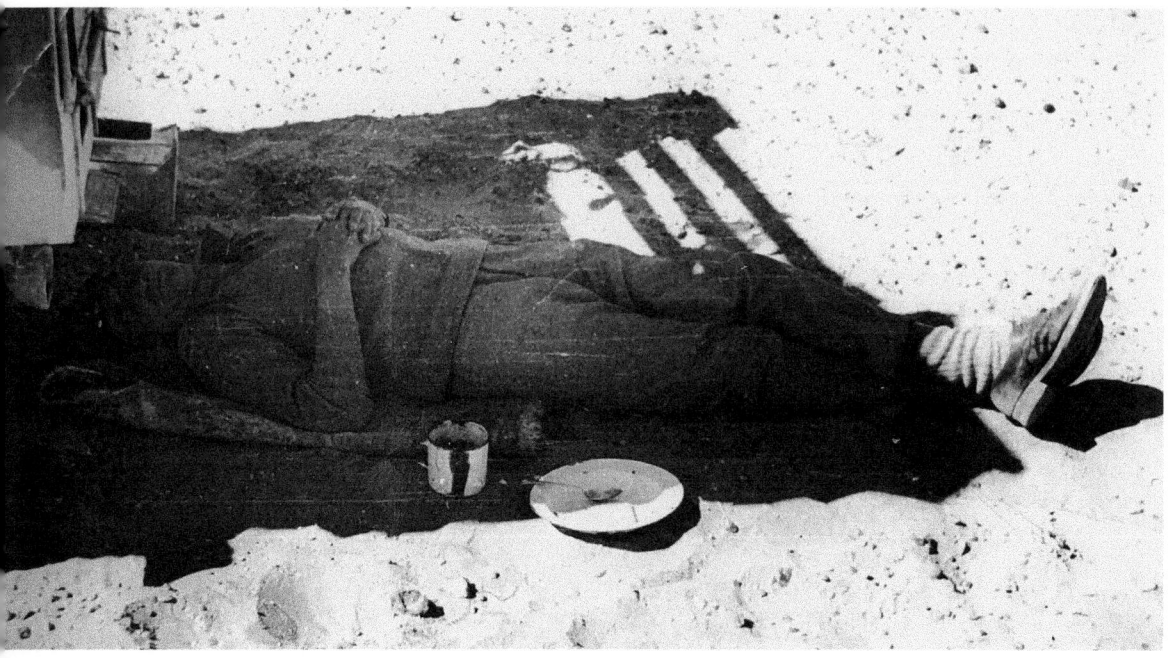

LRDG trucks parked alongside Cleopatra's cooling pool in Siwa.

T Patrol truck at Siwa. The sand channels have been employed to cross a drain. The locals look on.

An LRDG truck is greeted by Arab boys on donkeys as it approaches Siwa, most likely looking for an opportunity to barter.

R Patrol at the French fort at Zouar. From left: unidentified, Pte. G.H. Nelson, Pte. J.E. Gill, Gnr. C.O. Grimsey (navigator), Tpr. M.E. Hammond wearing French military dress, Sgt. C.G. Ball, Sgm. S.J.E. Mahomet (radio operator). On truck: Tpr. A.F. Dodunski, second right, Pte. E.B. Waetford, unidentified.

Commanders confer at Siwa. Left to right: Captain D. Lloyd Owen, Y Patrol; Captain J.R. Easonsmith, R Patrol; and Captain C.A. Holliman, S Patrol.

Members of G2 Patrol rest at Siwa between missions. Third from left, back row: Private N.A. Boyd, who was an RAOC fitter/armourer attached to G Patrol.

Kufra airfield and hangar captured by the Free French. The remains of an Italian Caproni Ca.309 Ghibli rest in the foreground.

Push-starting a Ford F30 alongside Kufra lake.

Wireless truck Y2, parked under the palms at Kufra. Note the wireless aerial in position. A camp has been set up on the right.

T Patrol men awaiting their Christmas lunch at Zella, 1942.

Troopers R.C. Davies (left) and T. MacDonald (right) enjoy a hot bath at the Zella oasis. It has been made from a cut-open Italian fuel drum with flimsy tins providing the walls. A fire was lit in a pit under the drum to warm the bath.

(**Above**) An unidentified trooper undertaking his ablutions. Water was strictly rationed.

(**Opposite, above**) A Ford 01 pilot car set up as a rest shelter. A sand mat has been wrapped around the base of the vehicle to act as a windbreak. Left: Signalman A. Pressick and Lieutenant S.W. Ellingham of T Patrol.

(**Opposite, below**) Y Patrol men rest among the scrubby dunes at Ain Ghetmir in February 1942. Captain D. L. Lloyd Owen is standing on the left in the sheepskin coat. Their well-loaded Ford F30 is parked behind them.

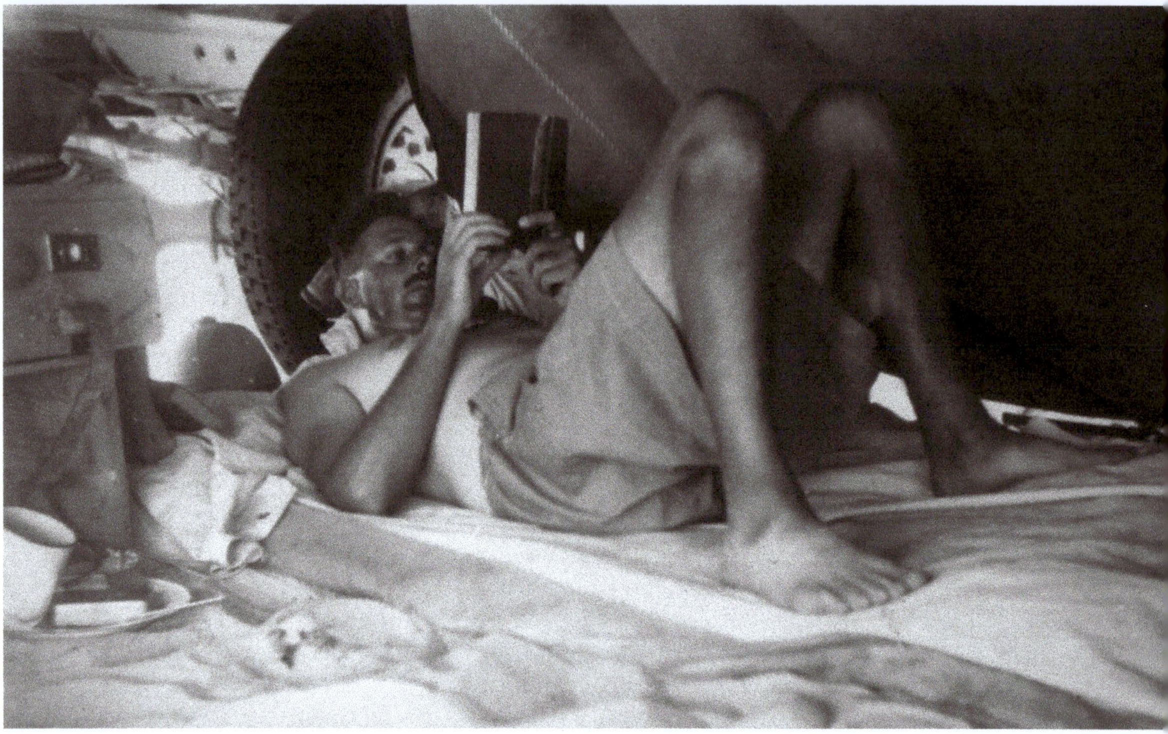

The heat during the day in base camps like Tazerbo and Kufra could become very oppressive in summer. The men spent time sheltered under the tarpaulins fixed to the side of their trucks. Here Lieutenant E.W. Ellingham rests in the shade, using the truck wheel as a headrest.

Y Patrol men enjoy a meal in an open field in the Mechili area. A sand mat provides a wind shelter for the resting place beside the truck.

S Patrol had established a comfortable camp at Zighen which they named the Rhodesia Club.

(**Opposite, above**) Y Patrol poses against their F30 truck. Note the number of men with bandaged desert sores, a common problem among the troops. From left: Lance Corporal A.S. Denniff, Trooper D.A. Hutchins, Trooper J.D. Hirst, Private R.N. Scott, Trooper A. Arger, Lance Corporal J. Miller-Kerr, Private S.J. Sandle, Trooper A.E. Bartliffe, Lance Corporal J.W. Carningham, Trooper H.C. Chard, Trooper G. Dawes, Sergeant Major K.L. Barbour, Lance Corporal S.M. Carr, Lance Corporal A.C. Graham. On truck, from left: Trooper A. Davis, Trooper H. Wise.

(**Above**) The LRDG established a base at Hon for a time.

(**Opposite, below**) T Patrol men visit Arab students at a school.

A patrol truck returns to the congestion of Cairo after a mission.

Trooper J.P.L. Macassey driving his Ford F30 in Cairo. He is accompanied by a man referred to as 'Le Caire' in the original photo.

Members of T Patrol enjoying a drinking session at the NZ Forces Club in Cairo, 1941. A number of Australian soldiers are also celebrating in the foreground.

A pamphlet promoting the Empire Hotel, a club for WOs, NCOs and men of the British Imperial Forces. It was further down the road from the Shepheard's Hotel, also close to the brothel district and Military Police station, should things get out of hand.

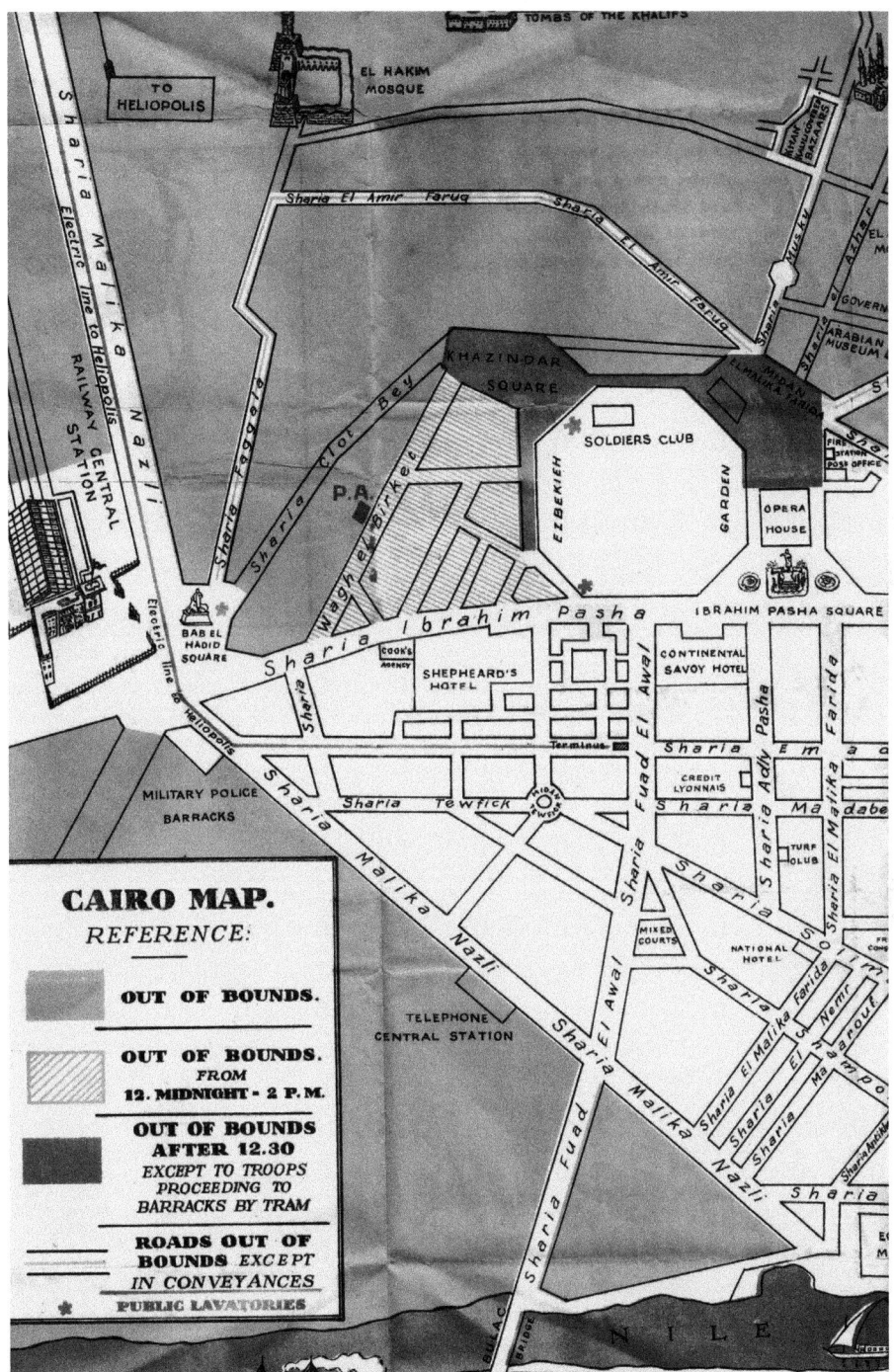

A wartime Cairo map issued by the military. It shows the 'P.A.', a prophylactic centre on the Wagh El Birket which was the official brothel area. After a long desert trip, the plan for many LRDG men was first off to the hotels for a nice meal and a cold beer, often followed by a visit to the brothels. All the soldiers' needs were located in a convenient central area.

A Stella beer advertisement from the *Parade* magazine. This beer was very popular with the troops after weeks on patrol. It was brewed from onions and commonly referred to as 'onion beer'.

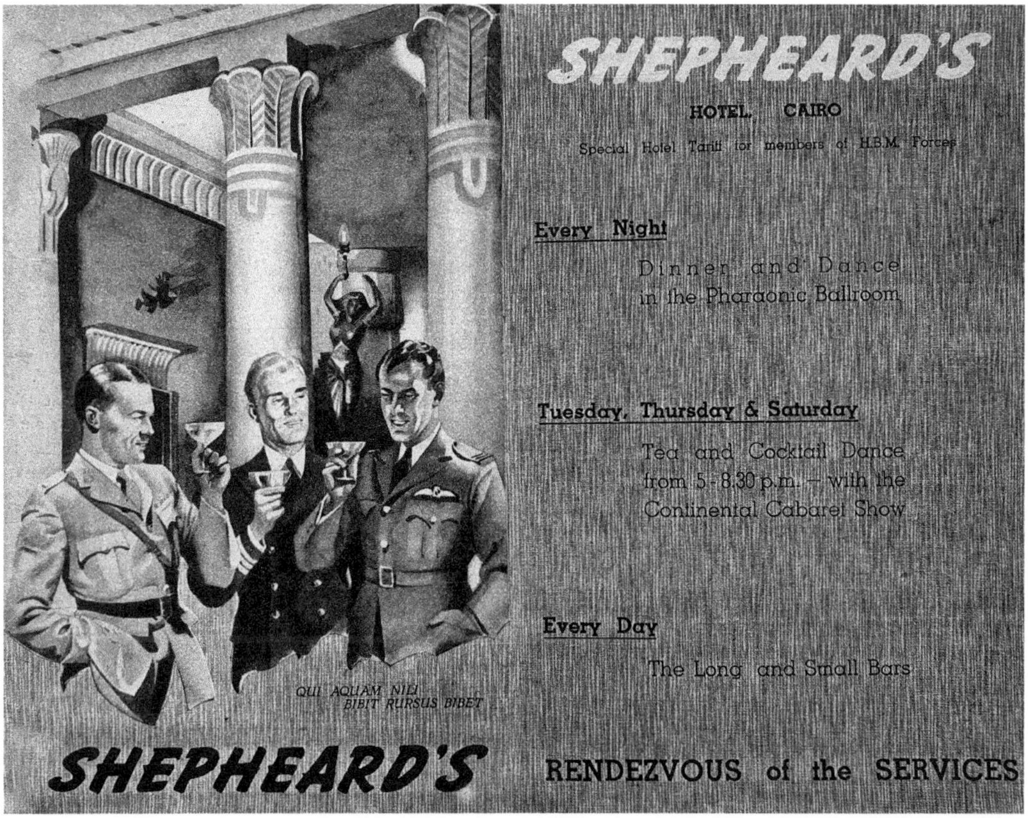

An advertisement from the wartime *Parade* magazine for Shepheard's Hotel in Cairo, a very popular venue for LRDG officers to relax.

T Patrol doing a Haka (a Maori war dance) before the commencement of a sporting event with S Patrol at the Rhodesians' desert base at Zighen in July 1941.

T and S Patrols playing basketball at Zighen. The goal posts mounting a cut out oil drum circle still stands today.

The troopers rest having dug out sleeping trenches for the night. A tarpaulin would then be placed over the holes to keep the sand out to make a cosy sleeping pit.

Chapter Ten

The Road Watch

In 1942 Rommel's Afrika Korps had broken out of El Agheila on the Gulf of Sirte in Libya and the Allies were desperately in need of reliable intelligence for their planned counter-offensive in Cyrenaica. To help gather this information the LRDG established the 'Road Watch'. This entailed the observation of the Tripoli-Benghazi road (*Via Balbia*), which was 643 kilometres behind enemy lines and was kept under constant twenty-four-hour watch over several months in 1942. It was along this road that the Axis forces brought almost all their armour, supplies and troop reinforcements. A large percentage of the information the Eighth Army received about enemy movements came via the radios of the LRDG stationed behind the lines.

The patrol would take up position 8 kilometres east of Mussolini's *Arae Philaenorum*, a grandiose stone archway straddling the highway which marked the demarcation point between Cyrenaica and Tripolitania. Known as the 'Marble Arch' to the Allies, it was built by the Italians as a monument to their colonization of Libya. The men first sought cover in shallow wadis in order to make camp and camouflage vehicles. Any wheel tracks that led to the wadi were carefully brushed out and small bushes were cut to adorn the camouflaged nets. A camp guard was always posted. Then before dawn each day two observers would select a hiding place about 270 to 370 metres from the road and conceal themselves in a fold in the ground or among the small scattered camel thorn scrub. They were provided with pencils, notebooks, compasses, powerful field glasses, a vehicle silhouette reference and rations including bully beef, biscuits and cheese, plus a water bottle that was buried in the sand to keep cool. Equipped in this way, they remained in place all day watching the traffic.

One man would be responsible for taking notes, while the other looked through his binoculars describing all transport going to or from the front. Personal weapons were not always carried, the principle being that if discovered, they could pass themselves off as scruffy, unarmed evaders from an overrun unit. Thereby the rest of the watch would then have a chance of slipping away elsewhere without interference, but there were other threats like road-workers and passing Arabs on camels. On one occasion a road convoy stopped and some soldiers fired their rifles at a herd of passing gazelle. However, it was in the same direction as the concealed watchers, so they had to keep their heads down until the danger had passed.

As stillness was the best camouflage, the observers could not move about much during the day except to roll onto their backs. When night fell, they were able to exercise more, not only to keep warm but to get closer to the road where they could judge the vehicles by their sound and outline. Just before dawn, having been replaced by two others, the two men would return to camp for a welcome breakfast and some rest. It was a very wearisome task, bitterly cold in winter, blowing dust in spring and blistering heat in summer; from dawn to dusk it was a very long day. It was considered one of the most unpopular jobs in the LRDG, yet was one of their most important.

The classification, markings, loads and other details of all troop and supply transport, ambulances, armoured vehicles and artillery were recorded as they passed. Even Allied PoWs were seen being trucked to the rear. Yet rescue was not an option, as the Road Watch could not be compromised. If the information was considered vital, it was immediately transmitted to LRDG HQ in Siwa. Otherwise it was sent when the patrol was relieved and clear of enemy territory. The intelligence gained proved invaluable to GHQ in Cairo in assessing the enemy's strength in Cyrenaica. It took three patrols to do this work. While one was watching the road for a week or ten days, the other was going out from the base at Siwa to relieve it and the third was making the 965-kilometre journey back. All the LRDG patrols shared this vital yet tedious work. This put a heavy drain on the unit and sometimes made it very difficult for them to carry out other tasks without overtaxing the men and trucks.

An insight into a routine Road Watch operation is provided in Operation Report No. 62, dated 16 November 1942, prepared by Lieutenant E.F. Spicer of Y1 Patrol. The task was to take a census of vehicles on the Benghazi–Tripoli Road, just east of Marble Arch, for a period from 23 October to 16 November 1942. The patrol consisted of one officer and eighteen other ranks with five trucks. The men were briefed by the Intelligence Officer in recognition of enemy equipment and vehicles and a supply of high-powered binoculars was drawn from stores.

From Kufra, rations for thirty days were taken, plus forty-five jerrycans of fuel per truck. These were to be refuelled at Zighen on the outward and return trips. Also an additional three cases per truck would be loaded from there for the outward journey.

The signal instruction was that any large troop movements had to be reported immediately, as would all armour if numbering above five in any period of twenty-four hours, plus any other information considered of extreme importance to be also sent by radio.

The patrol left Kufra on the afternoon of 23 October and arrived at sunset on the 29th without incident at Wadi Hatema, where a suitable place was found to make camp. On 30 October, the day was spent camouflaging their position and then reconnoitring a location for the actual watch, which began at 1900 hrs that evening.

On 7 November, Y1 Patrol was relieved by Lieutenant J.R. Talbot's R2 Patrol after a successful watch. Spicer's men returned to Kufra on 16 November. The trip was uneventful, apart from the following vehicle breakdowns, which included seven tyre blowouts and two damaged radiators. On 25 October, they had carburettor trouble with Y2, creating a three-hour job for the fitters. Two days later, it took another three hours to start the same truck due to the plugs oiling up badly.

The watch provided valuable intelligence based on vehicle movements to and from the front, with the report that listed ten detailed pages of road observations. However, there was one close encounter. Just after dawn, on the watch of Private F. Devine and Trooper A. Tanner, five Arabs mounted on camels rode past the men. Fortunately, they took no notice and did not attempt to go near the road to possibly warn the enemy.

Notable entries on the lists were nine trucks and trailers carrying approximately 300 British PoWs with motorcycle escorts, then on another day a further seven trucks and trailers carrying both British and Indian PoWs, along with three captured British Humber saloon staff cars and four trucks with trailers carrying dismantled aircraft. Trucks with trailers were also spotted carrying Italian troops who were singing and smoking!

An insightful overview of this work was described in the 'General Notes of a Road Watch' report written by Captain J.R. Easonsmith of R1 Patrol. This covered the watch period from 17 to 29 March 1942:

> Not a very high percentage of captured British vehicles were seen, probably 5 per cent. Those recognized were Macks, Whites or 3-ton Bedfords. The condition of this heavy transport appeared to be good and the littler stuff not noticeably bad. A great number of vehicles in the 3-ton and 30-cwt class had a white transverse bar about one foot wide painted across the radiator end of the bonnet. Some vehicles with cabs had stripes of green, white and red, each about one foot wide painted over the cab roof along the axis of the car. In the 10-ton and trailer class, many civilian lorries were being used for military purposes. They were painted in non-military colours such as in red and blue and had large names painted along the side of the body, such as Monti, U Signorette and Trucchi. Loads were difficult to judge, as easily 90 per cent of the traffic was covered and in most cases the back laced up. Quite a lot of loads of metal fuel drums were seen, but usually on 3-tonners. The bigger trucks and trailers were usually high-sided and when not covered the load was difficult to distinguish. Several loads of rough timber for fuel were seen going east. Vehicles going west were often empty. A common arrangement was to see a 10-tonner with an empty trailer loaded onto the truck and towing a second trailer with a truck on it.
>
> As so many of the largest convoys seen were about 20/25 vehicles, it looks as though larger numbers are split up and sent off at intervals. This was borne out by the arrival in sections of the convoy noted on March 21st. For the first couple of hours each morning, the preponderance of movement is westwards by a large margin. It seems probable that a lot of traffic reaches Agheila or thereabouts for a halting-point for the night. For two hours in the

middle of the day, traffic slackens off considerably. The busiest periods are 0900 hrs to 1030 hrs and 1330 hrs to 1530 hrs GMT daily. Very few trucks carried any form of AA defence that could be seen, but a lot had a man sitting in the back, probably as a spotter. Previous patrols have reported an armoured car patrolling the road. This was not seen during our stay. This task seemed to be carried out by Ghibli aircraft which flew on average at about 500 to 1,000 feet.

The condition of the road is maintained by gangs of Italian soldiers wearing uniform. They do not appear to be attempting any major repairs, but just stopping any serious deterioration, working in a different place each day. Parts of it are tar-sealed and parts stone and gravel finish. The telephone lines bear three lines.

Opposite to our camp on the northern side of the road, some vehicle pits had been dug, but were not being used. Similar pits were on the southern side of the road and at the base of the scarp in the Dor Lanuf area some 7 or 8 miles east of us. Nearly all the traffic at night used lights. No Arabs were seen in the area during our stay, but there were obvious signs that the camel tracks are well used at some periods during the year.

Though most Road Watch activities were uneventful and successfully accomplished, there were some in which the mission was compromised. One exceptional example is laid out in Operation Report No. 70 prepared by Captain J.A.L. Timpson of G1 Patrol, dated 29 December 1942. Their task was to carry out a traffic census on the coastal road west of Agheila. The plan was to relieve G2 Patrol which was currently undertaking the watch. The G1 personnel consisted of two officers and twenty other ranks, employing two jeeps and five 30cwt Ford F30 trucks. Each truck carried fifty-five jerrycans of fuel and eight jerrycans per jeep.

The patrol left Kufra on 20 November and the trip was uneventful until the 25th. That day at 9.00 am they spotted about a mile ahead eight Italian vehicles including two Autoblinda AB.41 armoured cars parked on the edge of an escarpment. The patrol wanted to avoid enemy action as their priority was to undertake the Road Watch. So they turned about and started to veer north, only to be confronted with another enemy force of five vehicles. Also at the same time the larger group started to drive towards the patrol. Firing soon began between both sides. One Italian vehicle caught fire from the guns of truck G1. Also G2 and G3 were inflicting damage to vehicles and personnel. The enemy then dismounted their vehicles and set up their weapons under ground cover. They also employed a mortar that mainly targeted three LRDG trucks that were bunched together.

Captain Timpson drove a jeep, while his gunner Corporal J. Wheatley operated the twin Vickers K alongside him. Timpson wrote of the action in his report:

> It was impossible to observe these trucks as I had plenty to do changing magazines on my jeep. After a few minutes of firing I tried to leave my

position to go over to the other trucks to get them to follow me in a breakout, but as soon as I turned the jeep round the enemy started to advance and move in to close the gap, so I returned and continued bursts of firing.

I could see that our right-hand trucks, after a good start when we seemed to put up plenty of fire, were now having a bad time. Gdsm. D. Hannah on G4 was seen doing good work firing his Vickers MG from the top of his truck and, when it jammed, he took over another water-cooled .50 Vickers gun behind the driver's seat. But his truck was seen to have had a bad knock from a shell of a largish enemy gun. After a while, most of the patrol had dismounted their weapons and were firing from the ground. It appears that our Breda gun never worked, though I was cheered to hear what sounded like it fire quite early on, but I was mistaken, it was apparently from an enemy gun. [Likely from the 20mm gun mounted on an Autoblinda AB.41 armoured car. The patrol Breda truck had been put out of action.]

Gradually the enemy was closing in on our right, and I went over to G2 and G3 and some men who had dismounted from the other trucks and told them to follow me in a break-out. I stopped behind the bank to give a last good burst at the enemy and then drove over it, making for the gap in the enemy's right. However, only G3 and G2 followed me out. Four enemy vehicles chased us for about 10 miles, but eventually stopped. I headed due north and then made several sharp bends. I passed through what I presumed to be their main post at Hofra, which was empty of enemy. All of them had, I suppose, gone to join in the fight.

After covering about 20 miles from the scene of the fight we lay up in a wadi for the rest of the day expecting enemy aircraft, but none appeared. I did not consider there was any chance of recovering the remainder of the patrol. The enemy was fairly close in when we left. Flight down the escarpment on foot would have been useless, since there was no cover and the slope was concave.

Despite the losses, Timpson was still determined to relieve G2 Patrol and take his turn on the Road Watch. Their strength was now reduced to himself, Lieutenant B. Bruce, Signalman H. Wheeldon and seven other ranks: Guardsman Anderson, Guardsman G. Blaney (the chief navigator), Lance Corporal F.A. Leach, Sergeant G.A. Ollerenshaw, Corporal J. Wheatley and Guardsmen A. Wilson and M.A. Welsh. They still had two Ford F30 trucks; fortunately one was the wireless truck G2 and the other G3, plus one jeep. Most of their supplies were gone in the three trucks and a jeep lost; however, they still had fuel for 550 miles and water and rations for twenty-four days. The cook's truck was gone, so no tea, sugar, oatmeal, milk and other provisions, including cigarettes that were particularly missed. They had also lost the fitter's truck, a problem if the Fords suffered breakdowns.

The patrol travelled from 26 to 29 November in search of G2, but when they arrived they found their camp had been evacuated only two hours before.

Nonetheless, near Wadi Zebaui they sought suitable cover for a camp from which to establish their watch. They immediately got the observation roster under way, with Timpson and Guardsman Welsh taking the first turn from a good position on top of a hill overlooking the road. From there the watch continued, but care had to be taken with the presence of both enemy and Arab camps and in the area of low-flying aircraft. There were some close enemy encounters, but they managed to evade them. They were also hampered by the discomfort of periods of heavy rain. On 7 December, Lieutenant Bruce's hand became poisoned by a thorn. It was swollen and he suffered a high temperature. The treatment was sulphanilamide pills taken internally. They were also ground up and spread on the infection, after which the wound was dressed. Signalman Wheeldon always remained at base while the others went on watch. He nursed Bruce and prepared meals, but spent most of his day working on the watch tallies, summarizing, encoding and transmitting signals.

On 12 December, an Indian Long Range Squadron patrol (I1 Patrol) under Lieutenant J.E. Cantley arrived at camp and brought fresh supplies including tea, sugar and cigarettes plus medical stores. Lieutenant Bruce would be stood down from the patrol and travelled with the Indian patrol for better medical care. On 13 December Timpson was advised by HQ that Captain Lazarus of S2 patrol was taking over the watch. On 15 December G1 Patrol, having fulfilled their mission over a very difficult fourteen days, set out for their base at Zella. He travelled with the Indian patrol that helped with petrol and rations. However, one of the surviving trucks, G3, that had provided good service throughout the operation, developed a faulty petrol system and was out of action for a good part of the day. Three days later the same truck broke its steering and, with the assistance of the Indian patrol fitters, took five hours to repair. The patrols finally arrived at Zella at noon on 20 December.

Timpson's devotion to continuing his watch despite the loss of the majority of his patrol was outstanding. This was reflected in the LRDG Operation Report, The Ninth Phase, 24 October 1942–23 January 1943 as follows:

> By this time, the importance of the Road Watch was more clear than ever, and it was decided to 'double-bank' the patrols in an attempt to maintain continuity at all costs. Therefore Timpson (G1) and Tinker (T2) left Kufra for this on 20 November. Both had trouble on the way north. The enemy was now fully aware of the use which we and the SAS Brigade were making of the Marada-Zella gap and they had laid mines and were maintaining patrols in it.
>
> On 25 November, Tinker lost a truck on a mine and one man had his leg broken. The following day, Timpson lost four trucks and twelve men in an engagement with an enemy patrol near Hofra. Tinker was ordered to return to Kufra with the wounded man, but Timpson continued with his reduced force, established a watch near Wadi Zebaui on 30 November and maintained it until 14 December. This was one of the outstanding achievements of

the LRDG. Everything was against Timpson, he had lost more than half his patrol, he was short of rations, the weather was vile, the area full of enemy troops and his other officer [Bruce] was ill with a poisoned hand.

Timpson was awarded the Military Cross, gazetted on 11 November 1943, for his devotion to duty in maintaining the Road Watch and under very difficult circumstances, while gathering valuable intelligence for the Eighth Army.

G2 Patrol Road Watch camp. The camouflaged trucks were well spread out.

Meal time at the G2 Patrol Road Watch camp.

T Patrol truck *Te Taniwha* well hidden while on watch.

The Y Patrol Breda truck concealed by bush and shrubs.

Trooper P.V. Mitford taking notes while observing the road.

R Patrol men preparing a meal while taking their turn on watch. The trucks are very well concealed. The man on the left with a pipe is Trooper J.A. Franks.

1900 hrs 1/11/42 - 1900 hrs 2/11/42

Observers: Tpr. LeGrice - Tpr. Patch.

EASTBOUND

M/Cycle & S/Car	1
30 cwt.	2
3-ton	20
3 ton & trailer	4
5-ton	29
5-ton & trailer	11
10 ton & trailer	2
	69

NOTES: 1 x 30 cwt. full of ITALIAN Soldiers. A convoy of 4 x 3 tonners and 2 x 3 ton & trailers passed just before dawn. 3 Chevs. & 1 Ford included in total of 3 tonners. 2 x 5 tonners and trailers and 1 x 10 tonner & trailer loaded with 40-gallon drums. 4 x 5-tonners loaded with very large wooden crates. 20 of the 5-tonners were 6/wheelers. 1 convoy of 15 x 5 tonners & 3 x 3 tonners. 1 x 10 tonner & trailer full of white sacks - probably cement.

WESTBOUND

M/Cycle	1
15 cwt.	1
30 cwt.	2
3-tonner	8
3-tonner & trailer	16
5-tonner & trailer	9
Tankers	1
Tankers & trailers	6
	44

NOTES: 1 x 3 tonner a Chevrolet. 2 x 3 tonners & trailers full of British P.O.W. 1 x 5 tonner & trailer loaded with 8 Breda 20 mm guns. 1 x 5 tonner & trailer with Volkeswagon on lorry and an Airplane refuelling tanker on trailer. Convoy of 7 x 3 tonners & trailers full of British P.O.W., approximate number 300., with 1 M/Cycle as escort & guards on each vehicle.

A Y1 Patrol Road Watch observation list report from 1/11/42 to 2/11/42, as taken from the Long Range Desert Group Operation Report No. 62, dated 18 November 1942 and prepared by Lieutenant E.F. Spicer.

Captain J.A.L. Timpson driving his jeep. In November/December 1942 while he was leading G1 Patrol they were attacked by the enemy while trying to establish a watch. Several trucks were lost but the mission was able to continue, despite the harsh conditions and limited resources.

An Italian Autoblinda AB 41 armoured car mounting a 20mm gun. Captain Timpson's G1 Patrol was attacked by these vehicles which knocked out several of the patrol trucks.

A captured photo of an Italian officer standing in front of the Italian monument the *Arae Philaenorum*, called the 'Marble Arch' by the Allies. This straddled the Tripoli-Benghazi road in Libya, which was kept under observation from March to July 1942. Note the fuel tanker and trailer travelling along the road.

In 1942 the Road Watch was established 8 kilometres from the 'Marble Arch'. This photo was taken in early 1943 with LRDG vehicles parked underneath.

Members of T2 Patrol pose at the base of the 'Marble Arch', 1943.

Chapter Eleven

Enemy Encounters

Generally the LRDG avoided close encounters with the enemy where possible. However, their most common danger was air attack, which accounted for most transport and personnel losses, with strafing usually being more effective than bombing. The best forms of protection if caught in the open were wide dispersion and concealment. With large stores of fuel and munitions carried on the vehicles, they were very vulnerable to enemy tracer gunfire.

One instance of an air attack was recorded in the LRDG Operation Report No. 69 by Lieutenant J.D. Henry, S2 Patrol on 27 December 1942. They were working with the Free French Forces at the time:

> At 0700 hrs our column was spotted by a Heinkel IIIK. We made for the escarpment to the east for cover and dispersed. The plane flew off. Four miles out we spotted two Italian Savoia [Savoia-Marchetti SM.79] bombers escorted by five CR.42 fighters. One fighter came to investigate our small party. He did some ground strafing, but was driven off by the three S2 Patrol trucks. The entire circus of planes concentrated on the column dispersed round the escarpment. The main attack seemed to be in the vicinity of our two wireless trucks that had separated from us. We completed our recce of the oasis and waited for the remainder of the column to join us in the oasis.
>
> Captain Carter [British Liaison Officer for Chad attached to S2 Patrol], who had remained behind with the wireless trucks, reported the HQ10 Chevrolet truck was written off by bomb splinters and ground strafing, and S9 was scarred but serviceable. Sgt. G.H. Jackson and Sgm. H.P. Du Toit were slightly wounded. Captain Carter was greatly impressed by Sgt. Jackson's coolness. Sgt. Jackson and Du Toit opened fire at the bomber and kept on firing until after the bombs left the plane and had passed, when he and Du Toit took cover under the truck, which was straddled by fifteen bombs; both were wounded. Sgt. Jackson then assisted Du Toit to the shelter of some rocks and dressed his wound during periodic machine-gunning of the truck crews by the fighters. S2 Patrol returned to the scene of the bombing to salvage what we could for spares. Removed one front spring, the remains of rations, W/T spares, gun magazines, etc.

Sergeant G.H. Jackson wrote his view of the action as an Appendix B to the Operation Report No. 69 as follows:

> On the morning of December 27th, the vanguard of the French Force took cover along the escarpment some 15 miles from the oasis of Magedul.

S2 Patrol, with the exception of the two W/R trucks HQ10 and S9, then accompanied the French Recce Patrol to make a recce of the oasis before moving the whole force into the palms.

Before the recce party had gone three miles the aircraft alert was sounded and five fighters and two bombers were seen heading for the trucks in the open. Du Toit and I stood to our guns on S9, the remainder of the crews taking cover behind some boulders halfway up the escarpment. The firepower of the recce party apparently drove off the planes as they turned and came straight for the escarpment. One Savoia headed for my truck. I fired until my gun was at maximum elevation and the tracer was going behind it. I then jumped down and flattened out in front of the back wheel. Du Toit got under the tailboard. We had no sooner got down than the bombs exploded. Something hit my shoulder and as soon as the smoke and dust cleared I made for the rocks where the others were. Du Toit arrived just after me. Shortly afterwards we saw a fighter dive and drop two bombs close to HQ10. The raid lasted approximately half an hour, planes bombing and machine-gunning the escarpment the whole time.

After the raid, Du Toit and I were sent to the Medical Officer. I left Du Toit there and returned to the trucks. HQ10 was damaged beyond immediate repair. S9 only had one wheel punctured, this had been exchanged with the only good wheel on HQ10 and as much of the kit as possible was salvaged.

Signalman Du Toit was initially given permission by the doctor to continue to walk about and undertake signalling. However, his wound became worse. The French medical officer ordered Du Toit to be evacuated to Zouar for an operation, as he thought a piece of bomb splinter was still lodged at bone level. Signalman T. Evans volunteered to take his place until a relief signaller could be obtained. However, four days later Evans developed 'telegraphist's cramp' and had to be stood down for a time.

Another air attack action took place in July 1942 against G2 Patrol, in which the commander Lieutenant Hon. R.B. (Robin) Gurdon received fatal wounds. The patrol had been working under the command of Major David Stirling of the SAS from their base at Bir el Quseir along with T1, G1 and Y2 Patrols and the Free French in raiding enemy transport positions and landing grounds. On 12 July, while operating in the area of Minqar Sida, G2 Patrol was strafed by three Italian Macchi fighters and Lieutenant Gurdon was mortally wounded and Guardsman E. Murray hit in the arm. The action was recorded by the G2 navigator Sergeant J. Stocker in Operation Report No. 50, 23 July 1942, which includes the following:

> The patrol trucks were made up as follows: G7 navigator, G8 patrol commander, G9 wireless truck, G10 cook's truck, G11 patrol sergeant and G12 Breda gun.
>
> At about 1700 hours the party was forced off the selected course by a low hill running east and west and proceeded on its south side for three-quarters of a mile until a very clear gap was found. Here on the south side a sand

dune was half-formed and the ground was sand hammocks covered with scrub. To the north, through the gap, the ground was almost flat and presented the appearance of an unfinished tarmac. The patrol leader [Gurdon in truck G8], on passing through, halted 400 yards on and called the navigator's truck [G7] alongside where their position and view was checked with the map. The remainder of the patrol filtered through and dispersed on the north side of the hill. The party was 17 miles short of their next objective and approximately 15 miles from the nearest L.G. At this moment [1715 hrs], three aircraft, subsequently identified as Macchis, were seen approaching from the west. The patrol leader endeavoured to avoid action by standing up and waving at the enemy, but following closer inspection, one plane cleared its guns overhead of trucks G7 and G8. Firing broke out from the rear trucks and under this cover an effort was made to move G7 and G8 from their open positions. Unfortunately G7 would not start and Lieut. Gurdon ordered his gunner and driver to temporarily abandon their vehicle and they all came on to G8. The navigator sat behind him on the spare wheel. The vehicle was being driven in eccentric swings between the planes towards the broken ground to the south. One Macchi was now placed in a good position for attack, firing all its guns at the front seats, from about 20ft high and 80ft away. The burst first caused the navigator to fall off, being hit very lightly, and he ran to a bush from where he saw Lieut. Gurdon fall off and run to another bush holding his stomach. The vehicle then stopped after 20 yards and continued to burn steadily. The planes continued to attack the other vehicles, which returned fire when the opportunity occurred. Shortly after 1800 hrs, the planes moved off to the north and all vehicles except G7 obtained cover in the shadow of the south side of the hill.

From information given by Cpl. J. Wilson, gunner to G8 and medical orderly to the patrol, Gdsm. E. Murray, who was the driver, was hit in the same burst and fell off and Wilson drew up the vehicle before proceeding to cover. The truck was further hit by the second Macchi and received three bursts in all. Cpl. Wilson and Gdsm. R. Harkness, the driver, started up G7 and moved over to the casualties. The navigator Sgt. Stocker went over at the same time and saw that Lieut. Gurdon had been badly hit and found Gdsm. Murray with a serious wound in his arm. He then directed Cpl. Wilson to Lieut. Gurdon and Murray with morphia obtained from G7, the patrol's medical kit having been burnt on G8. He also directed the Free French, who had then arrived, to Gdsm. Murray who removed him to cover. Shortly after, while Cpl. Wilson was still with Lieut. Gurdon, the planes returned and the driver took the vehicle away. The planes searched the south side of the hill, but did not see anything in the failing light and finally passed over Lieut. Gurdon and Cpl. Wilson without spotting them.

One truck was destroyed and there were no other casualties. Sergeant Stocker took over command and discussed with the Free French as to whether they should continue the mission. They even conferred with Gurdon, who was still clear-headed despite his suffering. He wanted his men to continue to go forward and attack the airfields. However, with the enemy now aware of their presence, the mission was most likely compromised. Consequently, despite Gurdon's wishes, the men decided it was more prudent to return to base as a whole unit and seek urgent assistance for the casualties. They travelled all through the night, but with the morning came fog, blinding the few landmarks that were there. However, at 1200 hrs the following day, Gurdon finally succumbed to his severe wounding and was buried with due honours by his G2 Patrol members among some dry limestone hills. An hour later the patrol met up with the SAS medical officer Captain M. Pleydell, who attended to Guardsman Murray. Sergeant Stocker's report continued:

> Cpl. Wilson and Gdsm. B. Vaughan [Gurdon's soldier servant] looked after Lieut. Gurdon throughout; he was entirely lucid and understood the actions taken by the party. This NCO reported the extent of the injuries to the MO which was caused by two cannon shells over the abdomen and one in the right lung. The MO stated on this evidence that it would not have been possible to have saved Lieut. Gurdon's life without an operation the previous evening.
>
> After a meal, the party proceeded to the main RV, where Murray under the charge of the MO was being operated on that night. His wounds were severe damage to the left elbow, with the bone joint still intact, and two bullet wounds in the right leg and a graze on the left leg.

The report mentioned Gurdon being hit by cannon shells, although the specific Macchi aircraft type was not mentioned in the report and both the Macchi C.200 and C.202 usually only mounted 12.7mm machine guns. So Gurdon was unlikely to have been hit by three cannon shells as such wounding would have been instantly fatal. On 15 July, the patrol left for Fayoum to meet the medical officer Captain R.P. Lawson and from there be transported by the LRDG ambulance truck. Murray, with his arm set in plaster, had to endure a three-day journey in the back of the wireless truck, G9. This included crossing the Qattara Depression, where the vehicles were getting stuck on a number of occasions. Meanwhile, Murray was made as comfortable as possible under the watchful care of the medical orderly Corporal Wilson. They finally met up with the medical officer and Murray was transferred to the Chevrolet ambulance truck and taken to LRDG HQ.

A further dramatic air attack account was described by Sergeant L.A. Willcox MM of R2 Patrol. This was recorded on 23 September 1942 as an Appendix to Operation Report No. 44 by Lieutenant J.R. Talbot, commander of R2 Patrol. Their mission was to patrol in conjunction with operations at Jalo by Z Force:

> 19 September 1942: Lieutenant Talbot stopped when he saw palm growth so presumed it to be the outskirts of Jalo. He then gave us the signal to advance.

Upon doing so I perceived Lieutenant Talbot running towards his truck and on looking up I saw one plane flying overhead; all trucks then scattered, as by this time five planes had spotted us and were coming in to attack.

There being no cover, we decided to make a running fight. On turning to scatter, I saw explosions on the skyline which I judged to be artillery fire from the oasis. This was later confirmed by other members of the party, definitely not caused by aircraft or bombing. We were then bombed and machine-gunned and with twisting and turning to avoid attack, we lost contact with the others. During this time our 20mm Breda, manned by Tpr. Campbell, opened up with good effect, after which four planes came in to attack, three machine-gunning and one bombing. We then found some small cover where we stopped, our gun being jammed. While Tpr. C.L. Fisher and Tpr. Campbell made for what little cover could be found, I tried to retrieve maps and escape kit, during which time we were being continually machine-gunned by four planes and during which I sustained a slight wound in my left arm.

This attack having lasted about an hour, the planes then disappeared, after which we decided to return to look for the other trucks. Following back on our tracks 5 miles we came upon R10 commanded by Tpr. A.F. Dodunski making towards us with the crew of the wireless truck, two of whom were wounded. We then decided to return to our cover to dress these wounded men.

L/Cpl. A.D. Sadgrove was wounded in the arm and leg, Tpr. Ellis wounded in the knee and Sgm. R. Atkins with a slightly injured back. We then washed and dressed the wounds with field dressings. Tpr. Dodunski had previously found cover and during the raid had seen planes diving and machine-gunning in the distance. After the raid, he made in this direction and found the wireless truck had overturned; here he had picked up the wounded and made in the direction of my truck. We had now three crews and two trucks, R7 and R10. We stayed in cover as the wounded needed attention. We kept a picket on until sunset as a lookout for other trucks or smoking vehicles. Nothing was seen. Also during this time planes continued flying overhead in relays of twos, presumed to be looking for us, but we were not spotted.

At sunset we all proceeded towards the wireless truck to salvage maps, theodolite, wireless set etc. On arriving at the vehicle we decided to upturn it and try to tow. We were hoping we could fix it to run by daylight. We spent about one and a half hours at the truck, during which time I was continually flashing prearranged signal 'R' with a torch, hoping to attract the attention of the other trucks, but without result. Not knowing our present position, we decided to head in the general direction of south-east with the wireless truck on tow. At midnight we hit Landing Ground 1. There, having fixed the wireless, we tried unsuccessfully to contact Kufra. We could not contact

Z Force or Y2 because the cipher was held by Lieutenant Talbot, who was missing, together with two other trucks, R12 and R8 and their crews.

On the morning of September 20, a plane was heard but not seen. The wireless truck was fixed and still unable to contact Kufra. I decided to make for Kufra with the wounded. On this run R7 jumped a razor-backed dune, causing head injuries to Pte. J.E. Gill and I suffered a cut in my back.

We finally arrived at Kufra on 21 September, 1700 hrs. In conclusion, I wish to make special mention of all personnel who, both under fire and later during our return journey and in spite of injuries, behaved with cheerful determination and willingness to get the party through.

Lieutenant J.R. Talbot concluded his Operation Report No. 44 with the following observation:

Personnel:
The spirit of the men of the patrol was excellent throughout the attack. No crew abandoned their vehicle while it was possible to keep up the running fight. I wish especially to mention the very fine work done by Sgt. Willcox in contacting two trucks, attending to the wounded men, recovering the truck which was overturned and getting the three trucks back to Kufra.

I also wish to bring to notice the excellent effort of Signalman R. Atkins who, although painfully injured when thrown from the truck which overturned, finally succeeded in getting his wireless set working and making contact with Kufra by emergency cipher. His devotion to work, his conduct and his cheerful personality are always of a very high order.

Casualties:
Evacuated to hospital: 4. Minor wounds: 3. Missing, believed safe: 3.

One unusual ground encounter with the Afrika Korps is recorded in the LRDG Operation Report No. 65 by Second Lieutenant K.F. McLauchlan, R1 Patrol, of an event that took place on 27 December 1942 while undertaking reconnaissance around the Gheddahia-Bu Ngem track. An extract of that report follows:

After lunch our intention was to proceed to Fortino and the South African captain was going to make a fix and if possible the patrol was going to recce the area to the west of the road. At 1545 hrs we were proceeding in desert formation, making our frequent close inspections of the area. Had just started moving again when I was told there was an A/Car [armoured car] coming up to us from the rear through the patrol. I stopped and stood up and saw a four-wheeled A/Car approaching about 50 yards from the rear. The commander had no hat on and was smiling, and I wrongly assumed he was from the KDGs [King's Dragoon Guards armoured cars]. As he drew alongside he picked up a rifle and covered the three of us in the truck. Then he ordered us in English to put our hands up! For a moment I thought it was a joke, but then realized the A/Car [an Sd.Kfz 222] was hostile.

The ambush was well-planned, but the execution as far as R1 truck was concerned was not well done. The A/Car had drawn up about five feet away from us and in the same axis. I concluded we had a reasonable chance of getting out and instructed the driver to drive on. This he did admirably and the A/Car manoeuvred to bring his 'fixed line' 20mm gun to bear upon us. The commander with his rifle was loath to pull the trigger on us until we had moved some five yards. They turned left to head us off, we turned right and then turned right around to make towards safe territory. As we swung we saw a similar A/Car alongside the W/T truck R2 and the entire personnel had surrendered.

We were chased for approx. two miles. The enemy scored a direct hit with a 20mm A.P. round and also succeeded in setting some baggage on fire. We crossed a wadi at 30mph and the enemy called it a day, contenting himself with having pot shots as we crossed the skyline. The following personnel were captured unhurt:

Capt. W.G. Alexander, South African Forces
L/Cpl. H. Norton (jeep driver), South African Forces
Gnr. C.O. Grimsey, LRDG R1 Patrol
Pte. K.C.J. Ineson, LRDG R1 Patrol
Tpr. R.D. Hayes, LRDG R1 Patrol
Sgm. T. Evans, LRDG R1Patrol attached

Losses:

One W/T 30cwt Chevrolet complete with signal instructions and ciphers.
Navigating equipment on R2.
One jeep and navigating equipment carried by Captain Alexander, South African Forces.

Both Italian and Afrika Korps armoured cars were always a threat to LRDG trucks and skilful manoeuvring was required to evade them. The following account relates an action in which two four-wheel-drive Sd.Kfz 222 Horch armoured cars mounting a 20mm gun and a 7.92mm MG 34 machine gun engaged S1 Patrol under Lieutenant K.H. Lazarus on 15 January 1942. They were on a topographical mission in an area of Tunisia working with Popski's Private Army (PPA) under Major V. Peniakoff and five of his men. The total force consisted of five trucks and two jeeps. On 6 March 1943, Lieutenant Lazarus wrote a full account of the action in his Operation Report No. 77:

15 January: Travelled up Wadi Zem Zem to where the patrol went into good cover of large sand hummocks and bushes. The OC [Officer Commanding, Lazarus] had gone ahead to the road to see if it was clear. At 0915 hrs, a mixed enemy convoy of about 50 vehicles came into sight, travelling north along the road to Mizda. OC returned to the patrol to warn them of the traffic on the road. The OC and one man then went back towards the road to find a place where the convoy could be observed for a good stretch in either direction.

The convoy by this time had passed. At 1030 hrs shooting could be heard down the road in the direction of the patrol. OC went back to where Major Peniakoff of the PPA had been watching the road. By this time, one patrol truck which had managed to cross over to the south bank on to open ground stopped and was under heavy fire from a point on the north bank.

This was the only vehicle in sight, except for a burning truck to the west. On investigation the burning truck was found to be a four-wheeled German armoured car [an Sd.Kfz 222 knocked out by the patrol] with a 20mm gun. This was the first indication as to the nature of the attacking force. By this time one Opel open car mounting LMGs (light machine guns) had reached the wadi bed and was firing from there at our truck.

On investigation, in the place where the patrol was lying up, three patrol vehicles were seen badly stuck in the sand, but none of the personnel were there. The enemy had by this time disgorged its infantry, who were keeping up a desultory fire at whatever they could see. There was no time to destroy the trucks, as voices could be heard in the vicinity and the enemy was moving down.

The OC decided there was nothing to be done at the moment towards assisting the patrol. So in two PPA jeeps, the party that consisted of the OC, Major Peniakoff, three other ranks and one Arab retired at 1115 hrs into some hills half a mile west of the main road. There the enemy could be kept under observation. They appeared to be making a thorough search of the wadi. The truck [S5] which was abandoned, stuck in soft ground, was retrieved by the Germans. As far as could be ascertained, the enemy patrol consisted of the following: Two four-wheeled Horch armoured cars (one destroyed by us). Six or seven heavy open cars, probably Opels and similar to that shown on page 99 of Target [an enemy vehicle recognition manual as used on the Road Watch]. The one which was seen at close quarters had mounted on it two LMGs and carried four or five men.

At 1600 hrs, the enemy patrol left the wadi and proceeded north along the Mizda road with four of S Patrol's 30cwt Chevrolets. At sunset our small party went back to the scene of the action. There we contacted Cpl. C.C. Ryan and seven men, who had been hiding in a scarp. The only vehicle that was saved was S2, the wireless truck which was driven by Pte. J. Brannigan. He is to be commended for his good driving in getting his truck across the wadi and into broken hill country.

After Brannigan had driven his truck into the hills, he and two others, Pte. A. Bond and Pte. A.F. Goddard took some rations and water and went off by themselves to get further away from the enemy in the wadi. Cpl. Ryan, L/Cpl. T.J. Lewis, Pte. A.E.F. Bailey, Pte. A.T. Low, Sgm. C.H. Whitehead, the medical orderly, wireless operator and one PPA Arab stayed in the vicinity of the truck until nightfall and then came back to the scene of the action.

The wireless truck was then brought down to the wadi. After waiting for stragglers until 2300 hrs, the party, with two jeeps and one 30cwt, proceeded down the wadi to our camp of the previous night. There we met Sgt. R.B. Low, Pte. Spencer and one PPA man. Gnr. E.J. Henderson was known to have been badly wounded (he later died).

Pte. Sheeky of the PPA would not accompany the other men who escaped into the hills when the truck S5 was stuck in soft ground, but was content to await capture. At this stage, the men who could not be accounted for were Brannigan, Goddard and Bond (after a remarkable ten-day 300-mile trek, they finally arrived at Hon). We waited for two days for the above men to turn up, but as they did not arrive by the afternoon of the 17th, the party moved 10 miles south-east.

From the 18th to 21st the party made its way to a point on the road 30 miles south of Sciueref and there met Lieut. Tinker of T2 Patrol on the 21st. The party, now less the PPA, then accompanied Y2 Patrol to Hon, arriving there on 22 February.

The story of what happened to the three trucks of S1 Patrol caught in the wadi was later related by Private Alexander Bond who escaped from there. The men were resting and enjoying a fresh brew of tea when Sergeant R. Low spotted a German column coming their way. The men immediately jumped to their trucks and manned their weapons. A German Sd.Kfz 222 armoured car opened fire with its 20mm gun, but at the same time Lance Corporal T. Lewis returned fire with his .50 Browning, setting the enemy vehicle on fire. Unsettling the Germans, the remaining vehicles turned around and scattered, but the soldiers left the vehicles and sought cover in the wadi. They set up their machine guns and fired at the trucks that were still exposed in the middle of the wadi. Their fire was accurate and the Chevrolets were getting shot to pieces. Some were disabled by tyres being blown out, then another Sd.Kfz 222 appeared on the scene firing its 20mm gun and 7.92mm machine gun. At that moment the men decided to abandon their vehicles and make for what little cover there was. In doing so, Gunner E.J. Henderson was hit in the legs and collapsed where he fell.

While the men were under cover, Henderson bravely gave a running commentary to his comrades on the movements of the enemy. The men wanted to return to the trucks to get morphine for him, but he said it would be hopeless to cross that open ground under fire. Henderson urged his comrades to make a run for it away from the wadi. He shouted that his wounds were fatal and he was done for. The men ran towards some small hills, initially escaping over some exposed landscape with bullets spraying all around them, but miraculously they managed to reach better cover unscathed. They hid in some small hills where they were safe and could rest for a time.

Severely wounded, Henderson was uplifted by the Germans, but did not recover and died sometime afterwards. Later his grave was found clearly marked where the Afrika Korps had given him an honourable burial. Wandering tribesmen reported that a volley had been fired over his grave and that the German officers had saluted it.

(**Above**) An Italian Lancia truck being recovered by two Chevrolet WA trucks after running over a mine.

(**Opposite**) An LRP photo of a British Vickers Mk VI light tank displaying a trophy of a cut-out swastika centre of a large Nazi flag.

(**Below**) A Fiat 508 Militare convoy escort vehicle captured by the LRDG. The large cognac brandy barrel would have impeded the effective use of its defensive machine gun. This indicates that they were not anticipating enemy action.

Italian Fiat 508 Militare convoy escort vehicle on fire following an LRDG attack. A Ford F30 is on the right.

G2 Patrol trucks G11 and G7 parked alongside a burned-out Heinkel He 111. The Luftwaffe squadron has been identified as the 4th *Staffel* (2nd *Gruppe*) of *Kampfgeschwader* 26. II/KG26.

A photograph captured by the LRDG of relaxed-looking Italian soldiers.

A burned-out Italian Carro Armato M13/40 medium tank. It was armed with a 37mm gun and twin 8mm machine guns.

A patrol assembles in front of the abandoned Italian fort of Bir es Sciueref. This was situated along the road from Sebha to Tripoli.

General Erwin Rommel in a Caproni Ca.309 Ghibli ('Desert Wind') aircraft. The pilot was Vittorio Bosdari, an NCO pilot of 23 *Squadriglia 2 Gruppo Presidio Coloniale*. Between 19 February and the end of July 1941, he was attached to the Afrika Korps to fly Rommel and other German officers around the desert battlefields. This aircraft was a general-purpose light reconnaissance bomber. It was encountered by the LRDG with air attacks on a number of occasions.

Using a vehicle as a table, General Rommel confers with Luftwaffe officers during the Libyan campaign.

A Caproni Ca.309 Ghibli on fire following an LRDG attack.

An abandoned Fiat SPA TL.37 being examined by a trooper. Left: a wheeled 20mm Breda Model 35 gun.

LRDG men endeavour to recover a bogged Afrika Korps Horch staff car.

British officers examine a captured *Sd.Kfz* 222 armoured car. Armed with a 20mm gun plus a machine gun, these vehicles had a number of encounters with LRDG patrols.

A downed Heinkel He 111 Luftwaffe bomber. When Kufra was raided on 25 September 1942, five out of the eight Heinkel bombers were shot down by LRDG and SAS vehicle-mounted weapons.

LRDG men at Tobruk pose alongside a German 88mm flak gun.

A British M3 Grant tank totally destroyed by a direct hit, most likely a victim of an Afrika Korps 88mm gun.

Captain N.P. Wilder's truck *Tutira III* in Italian hands, September 1942. It was abandoned in Barce town after crashing past two enemy L3 light tanks. Note the ripped off mudguard.

The Italian L3 CV-35 light tank. They had a crew of two and were armed with twin 8mm machine guns. The LRDG encountered these small armoured vehicles a number of times, especially during the Barce raid in September 1942.

An Italian Carro L6/40 light tank. The LRDG came across many abandoned battlefield vehicles from both sides.

An Afrika Korps Sd.Kfz 15cm self-propelled field howitzer.

Italian Pavesi P4 artillery tractor; note the large tyres. Photo from an LRDG captured Italian camera.

A Savoia-Marchetti SM.82 transport/bomber found by the LRDG crash-landed in the desert. The windscreen shows signs of battle damage. A grave and a mangled body were found alongside this aircraft.

The captured Italian airfield at Castel Benito. Most of the aircraft in the foreground are Macchi C.200 Saetta fighters. This aircraft type shot up patrols on a number of occasions.

Members of the Afrika Korps examine a crash-landed RAF Curtiss P-40 Kittyhawk fighter. It was from aircraft like this that the LRDG recovered the .303 Brownings from the wings and converted them into truck-mounted machine guns.

An Italian Fiat CR.42 Falco fighter abandoned at Saloum after a forced landing, 1942. In the desert operations, these aircraft successfully attacked LRDG patrols on a number of occasions, resulting in fatalities and the loss of vehicles.

Chapter Twelve

The Libyan Taxi Service

As masters of desert travel and navigation, the LRDG was often asked to guide others to their objectives. These included units like the SAS, the Libyan Arab Force, the Free French, the Sudan Defence Force, Middle East Commandos and the Inter-Service Liaison Department (ISLD). Furthermore, they undertook other tasks such as inserting, supplying and collecting British and Arab undercover agents, recovering downed aircrew and rescuing Allied prisoners of war. They also carried army and RAF observers to reconnoitre the suitability of the landscape for future advances or for landing grounds. Other guests were taken who wrote of or painted the LRDG experience such as the British war correspondent Richard Dimbleby and New Zealand war artist Captain Peter McIntyre. The Group referred to this transport activity as 'The Libyan Taxi Service'.

In their courier role, as experts in the field of desert survival, geography and navigation, they were able to drop off or pick up men from far behind the lines, which for the most part was done without being detected by the enemy. Insertion by air or sea would have provided a greater risk for these parties. More than eighty men from various organizations were carried from 1941 until the end of the desert war. During these trips only four passengers are recorded as being killed while operating with the patrols.

To discover all they could about the enemy, British agents enlisted the support of friendly natives and lived as Arabs among the tribesmen of Jebel Akhdar, while transmitting information by wireless. The LRDG took the agents deep behind enemy lines and delivered their wireless batteries, equipment and supplies as required; sometimes to a place where they could complete their journey more discreetly by camel or on foot. One example of such a trip was in August 1942 when R1 Patrol took a party of three agents from Kufra to Bir Tala, about 190 kilometres to the south-east of Tripoli. Three months later the same patrol repeated the 3,200-kilometre return trip to deliver stores and to relieve the wireless-operator, who had become very ill with desert sores all over his body.

In August 1941 Major D.G. (Don) Steele was appointed the commanding officer of A (NZ) Squadron LRDG. He was awarded the OBE in recognition of his services while in command at Siwa and later Jalo. Steele had planned operations that included successful attacks on enemy communications and airfields, reconnaissance as far as Tripolitania and the transport of demolition parties, secret agents and search parties to various points behind the lines. In 1949 he wrote his recollections of the 'Libyan Taxi Service':

> The 'Taxi Service', so-called, was run mainly between Siwa and the Jebel Akhdar. Many gallant souls in Egypt, who spoke fluent Arabic, had joined the General Service branch of the ME Force in Cairo and had suggested the idea of installing themselves with some of the Arab tribes to find out what they could about the enemy and also to enlist the help of friendly natives. They were very brave men. They lived as Arabs and were in constant danger of being betrayed and shot by a realistic enemy. Such information as they obtained was sent back by radio. They had sets buried in all sorts of places. Our job was simply to take them where they wanted to go and later bring them back. In between times we would take them food for distribution among the natives, batteries for their radios and ammunition and explosives. They had nice habits, those men, and liked nothing better than to play tricks on the opposition. One never knew what was going to turn up on those trips. Aircraft of both sides were often about and both were hostile. Enemy ground patrols were regularly in the Jebel area and had to be avoided at all costs so as to not to give the game away. Sometimes the Arabs would bring an escaped PoW to the rendezvous and the patrol would have the pleasant job of delivering him safely to his own mates again.
>
> Returning from one such run, a patrol got a bad fright. They were steaming along headed for home when someone cried 'Aircraft!' Several fighters were coming along at zero feet almost on their track. There is nothing worse than a fighter at zero feet if you are in a truck and he sees you. However, the planes disappeared over a ridge and appeared to land. Curious, the patrol poked its head over the ridge too and they saw a plane on the ground. They went to investigate, where they found an RAF crew of a Wellington bomber that had been winged over Benghazi and made a forced landing. They were walking home and seemed glad of the offer of a lift by the patrol. Amazingly, there was a New Zealander among them, Lindsay Grey, who I had known as a boy!
>
> Our other 'taxi' tasks were almost without exception quite interesting. In fact, any old job that was required well into enemy territory, and some of them were very odd jobs. When the first Flying Fortress bombers came to the Middle East they were stationed near Cairo (all three if I remember). One day a frantic message came from the Army to say that one of the precious machines had made a forced landing west of the wire and would we rush out and demolish the bomb sight. It was all most urgent as the enemy did not know the principle of the instrument and must be prevented from getting it. Hurry, hurry, hurry! Out went the patrol, spent a couple of days getting to the general area, then half a day searching for the plane, only to find that the 'drop the bombs in a pickle barrel' sight had been destroyed by the crew before they left.

In 1981, Patrick McGraith wrote in the *LRDG Association Newsletter* an account of a trip in which he carried a British agent behind the lines and the difficulties encountered along the way. McGraith was the first commander of Y Patrol:

> I was ordered to take a British agent, Captain Taranto, up to the Gebel, south-east of Slonta some 200 miles with enemy-held territory to rendezvous with a pro-British Arab sheik. I took five trucks and, much against my better judgement, permitted Taranto to take with him his undesert-worthy and spareless light van which he wanted to use when he arrived up there to save himself a long walk in the desert heat.
>
> The outward journey of over 350 miles took two and a half days of hard driving. Added to this on the first night Taranto produced a bottle of Weasel brand gin which appeared to be pure alcohol and that in crossing an unavoidable and notoriously difficult area of rock and stone, we broke five or six main springs and thus used up all the spares we carried. But we arrived in the hills of the Gebel without incident. We leaguered at a point in the hills beyond which we could go no further due to fearful going. I agreed to Taranto's request for a volunteer fitter to accompany him on his mission. But I would not agree to his suggestion that they both dressed up in German helmets and jackets which we had found amongst the debris of earlier battles on our way up. To have done so would have risked death as spies had they been captured.
>
> Taranto then set off, saying that he would be returning in three days. Our leaguer, although fairly well hidden, was one from which it would not have been easy to fight our way out had we been spotted either from the ground or from the air. My anxiety was increased when Taranto did not return by the end of the third day. I began to suspect that he had been captured. But I decided to wait a further 24 hours.
>
> On the fourth day Taranto and the fitter returned on foot, exhausted. The van had been irreparably damaged. Taranto had got lost on his way to find the sheik. To prevent further delay, he had been compelled to ask the way from an Italian soldier and thereafter to drive a considerable distance along the main road, mingling with enemy convoys.
>
> I was most anxious to leave, for had we stayed long enough there was the risk of being given away by hostile Arabs or otherwise discovered. Furthermore, my medical orderly had a temperature of 105 and another soldier a temperature not much lower and both were delirious. But before leaving, we were compelled to move across very difficult country to the abandoned van to camouflage it and pinpoint its position for collection by the next patrol to visit the area.
>
> An hour later, on re-entering the rock and stone area my truck broke a mainspring. With no further spares its abandonment seemed inevitable, but my patrol sergeant, who was a skilled and ingenious fitter, bound and wedged the spring with leather bootlaces, wire, metal and wood. He told me

to stop every quarter of an hour so that he could tighten the makeshift contraption. He bet me a bottle of whisky he could get the truck safely back to Siwa if I did so.

The constant halts to attend to the spring and to the delirious patients were most tedious. The return journey was otherwise uneventful, except I was lucky enough to get within 30 yards of a black panther and her three cubs. This was the second time within a few weeks that a black panther had been seen by an LRDG patrol and it was confirmation that these rare, swift and graceful creatures were not, as hitherto believed, extinct in the Western Desert.

We duly arrived safely in Siwa and my patrol sergeant received his bottle of whisky. We were all bearded and scruffy, but a beard protected one's face from the intense heat, wind and dust. To those at base we stank most fearfully on returning from any but the briefest patrol and sometimes I had to burn my clothing!

Major Steele had also worked closely with Major David Stirling in planning combined operations. He respected their work and wrote of his time providing transport for the SAS:

The Special Air Service, 'Parashots' to us, were a tough lot of thugs. Their delight was to be dropped on some enemy landing ground or other objective, do what damage they could and then take their way home best they could. This was not very satisfactory for several reasons. First, as it was essential to the success of their operations that they be dropped at night, it was almost impossible for the RAF to drop them in the right place owing to the difficulties of navigation in an aircraft in darkness. Second, it was impossible to predict conditions on the target. And lastly, there was the problem of getting home. No unit can afford to lose half of its highly-trained men in each operation. We first met David Stirling and his merry men after they had made a raid on the landing ground at Ain Gazala.

It was one of those shows where everything goes wrong. Only some of the planes had found the target and of the men who landed on or near the aerodrome some were lost or drowned when they landed in a wadi which was running bank high with water from a sudden rainstorm some distance inland. We had been told to RV with the SAS men at a point to the south of the field. This we did and brought what remained of the party back to Siwa. Stirling was so impressed with the 'line of shot' about being able to go to any point with absolute certainty that he suggested that we should carry his men into their future tasks. On his return to Cairo he was able to arrange this and later the patrols were to go on many jaunts with these desperados. They too were very nice men and very brave, but they had strange ideas of fun.

Gunner C.O. 'Bluey' Grimsey was the navigator of R Patrol under Captain J.R. Easonsmith who provided pick-up and transport for the SAS mission where the men attempted their first parachute jump into their targets. However, they were dispersed by an unpredicted storm. Grimsey wrote a diary account of the rescue events in which he refers to the SAS as 'paratroopers':

> On 17 November 1941, we left Siwa at 0700 hrs and set out for the Libyan border with six 30cwt trucks under Captain Easonsmith to pick up a party of paratroopers on their way back from a demolition stunt. These men take extreme risks to destroy aircraft and ammunition dumps.
>
> This particular group under Captain Stirling was to attack at three different points hundreds of miles behind enemy lines and to make their raids in the dead of night on five aerodromes at Timimi, Gazala and Martuba. Luck was against them for a start. They were dropped in the dead of night, but encountered a 25mph wind and heavy rain, conditions that were not expected when they set out from the Eighth Army at Bagush. Some of the paratroopers were dragged and badly knocked about when they landed and their explosives got wet through. One party found it impossible to cross a wadi which had become a raging torrent below an escarpment which bordered the objective. Another party was dropped about 40 miles from the right spot. I do not know what became of the other parties.
>
> On 19 November, we proceeded north and slightly east to El Teilim where we camped for the night. Two dimmed lanterns were set in the hills by our camp. In the event of them getting away, the paratroopers were to make for this rendezvous, some 40 to 50 miles from their operation area. We were to give a signal by swinging these lanterns from side to side. Our patrol kept an all-night picquet. The password was the tune *Roll Out The Barrel*, sung or whistled. At 2150 hrs a sergeant called out that the lights were swinging and a few moments later there came floating across the still night the password tune. Otherwise there was not a sound, for we were deep in enemy territory and sitting alongside one of their main roads, from Mekili to Bir Hakim.
>
> We picked up seventeen men that night. They were cold and hungry after their trying ordeal and long trek. We made them as comfortable as we could with a tot of rum and all the bedding at our disposal. The next morning we picked up a few more and after spending the greatest part of 20 November in the vicinity we left for Gueret el Halib with twenty-one additional men to our normal complement and we stayed a night and a day there.
>
> We received news by wireless code to contact that other half of R Patrol, under Lt. Tony Browne located on the desert road junction of Bir Tengeder. On the way to this place we were sighted and attacked by an Italian Savoia SM.79 heavy bomber which machine-gunned us before it flew off. For two days we tried unsuccessfully to contact the patrol. At night we heard distinctly heavy bombing 50 to 60 miles to the north and could see the flames hanging like stars on the distant horizon. Planes searching for us flew overhead.

Eventually we decided to return to Giarabub with the paratroopers. We were surprised to be stopped on the way back by Tony Browne's patrol who had seen us machine-gunned two days earlier but failed to attract our attention. The twenty-one paratroopers we rescued had no bedding, very little clothing and practically no food. Each meal was an entertainment and we had to smile at the sight of Captain Stirling eating porridge off a piece of board and using another piece of wood from a benzine box as a spoon.

What became of the other over fifty men who were dropped that night I do not know, but it is to be hoped some of them made their way to the coast or were able to make the second rendezvous at Fraser's camp at Gueret el Halib. There is little doubt that some of them must have fallen into enemy hands. Those we contacted were tough and were looking forward to their next job when, they said, they hoped we could meet again.

25 November: At last we arrived back at Giarabub in the afternoon. It was a great relief, for it had been a responsibility careering about in enemy territory without lorries loaded with men who were ill-equipped to assist us in an emergency. As it happened, the truck in which I was travelling turned over at high speed, but by some miracle no one was seriously hurt. Later I learned that one party of paratroopers did succeed in getting onto an enemy landing ground and destroying many planes there.

The co-operation between the paratroops and the LRDG proved so successful that a further raid was made when S Patrol under Captain Gus Holliman took Commandos to a spot where they destroyed planes on the ground and escaped without casualties. Captain Holliman was awarded the MC. It seems that our method of dropping these men safely at the right place is better than dropping them by parachute, where invariably equipment is lost and injuries cannot be avoided.

On another 'Taxi Service' mission, an R1 Patrol operation under the command of Captain L.H. (Tony) Browne took place between 12 and 30 November 1942. The task was to transport an undercover radio-operator along with 998 kilograms of stores for his hideout at Bir Tala, 1,600 kilometres from their starting-point at Kufra. The patrol consisted of six Chevrolet patrol trucks with two officers and fifteen other ranks. In addition, travelling with them was an observer, Captain M. Pilkington of the Life Guards attached to the Arab Legion, acting as Intelligence Officer.

Captain Browne recorded the mission in his Operation Report No. 49 dated 2 December 1942:

> The patrol left Kufra at 1500 hrs on 12/11/42 and arrived at Tazerbo Landing Ground at noon the following day. Here petrol containers were refilled from an existing dump. The journey continued without incident until the morning of 16/11/42. At about 0900 hrs the patrol was crossing the Kufra depression. On rounding the western end of a large rocky hill, I saw six to seven men and two vehicles in a cleft in the hill about 40 feet up.

At least two machine guns were ground-mounted. It appeared to me that they hoped we should not see them and that either they had laid mines further on, or intended to open fire when all our trucks were in view. Consequently, as there was a wadi offering good cover about 800 yards to westward, I swung gradually round with the object of disguising the manoeuvre as one not caused by my having seen the enemy post. Fire was opened by the enemy when only two of our vehicles had reached cover. We replied while still on the move with accurate shooting, particularly by our .50 Browning gunner, who caused the enemy to take cover.

I then ordered my Breda truck to take up a strategic position in the wadi and to attempt to dislodge the enemy from their post. About a dozen trays [12 × 20mm rounds per tray] were fired and by observation the range was found and the shooting appeared to be excellent. It was obvious, however, that a serious attempt to take the position would involve loss of much time and the risk of jeopardising the success of the task. Therefore, I decided to continue northwards and signalled the necessary information to Group HQ. It has since been ascertained that the two enemy vehicles were put out of action by our fire.

On the morning of 17/11/42 we arrived at a prearranged RV, where we were joined by Y2 Patrol and a detachment of the Heavy Section. After refilling with petrol we continued north-westward, having arranged to meet Captain Hunter [Captain A.D.N. Hunter] with Y2 in the Wadi Tamet. Shortly before reaching the wadi we were seen by a Ghibli recce aircraft. There are steep cliffs on either side of Wadi Tamet and each of my vehicles selected a cleft with bonnets facing downhill. Half an hour after our arrival a Heinkel flew over and was then joined by two Capronis which flew round in a wide circle but took no action. At about midday several CR.42 Italian fighter aircraft arrived and machine-gunned our vehicles half-heartedly. All our guns were firing and none of the enemy pilots seemed disposed to make a determined attack. About 1230 hrs all the aircraft disappeared and I took the opportunity of moving my vehicles to new positions.

Within half an hour a larger number of CR.42s arrived [fourteen were counted]. At least two of these disregarded our fire and low-level attacks were made. During these attacks it is regretted that Captain M. Pilkington, Life Guards, and Lance Corporal N. O'Malley, NZEF, patrol navigator, were mortally wounded and died within two hours. Both men were shot while firing machine guns. Private M.F. Fogden, NZEF was shot in the legs. The W/T and patrol commander's truck were both damaged beyond repair. At dusk Captain Pilkington and Lance Corporal O'Malley were buried in one grave on the western side of the wadi.

The patrol was divided into two parties, each having two trucks. One party commanded by me was to continue to the destination and complete the task, the other commanded by Sergeant R.J. Landon-Lane to return to Kufra with the wounded man, Private Fogden. Having stripped the two damaged trucks and transferred the W/T sets, the two parties set off in opposite directions at about 2200 hrs. Sergeant Landon-Lane's party returned to Kufra without incident, Private Fogden having been collected from Tazerbo by air.

My party drove westward from Wadi Tamet for five hours during the night of 17/18 November and halted in thick tall bushes. The natural camouflage was excellent and searching aircraft failed to locate us. We continued westward at 1500 hrs on 18/11/42 and crossed the Hon-Misurata road. The following day we again laid up until the afternoon. After continuing for 20 miles the going became very bad and movement at night was not considered advisable.

We arrived at our destination at sunset on 20/11/42. It was found, however, that we had approached the RV by a wadi too far north which debouched on to the Bir Tala Landing Ground. As the actual RV was at the top of an escarpment some 500ft above, it was necessary for us to find a track up the cliff. A native guided us to a narrow camel track and during the night of 20/21 November under a high moon, we widened the truck and built it up where necessary so that the trucks could ascend. We reached the actual RV where Major A.I. Guild had dropped his men last August at 0500 hrs on 21/11/42. We left for the return journey at 1000 hrs on 21/11/42. We crossed the Misurata-Hon road and Wadi Tamet without incident. As we had extra petrol from the two abandoned trucks, it was found unnecessary to refill at the Heavy Section dump.

On the evening of 23/11/42 we were observed by two enemy fighter aircraft. It was already dusk and they made off in the direction of Zella. We continued southwards without further incident, arriving at Tazerbo on 28/11/42. Here we met by arrangement the LRDG aircraft for the purpose of evacuating the Sudanese W/T operator whom we had brought from Bir Tala. He was suffering from desert sores and weakness due to undernourishment. We arrived at Kufra at dawn on 30/11/42 after a 1,017-mile journey. There were no mechanical breakdowns on the journey and few punctures and blowouts due to excellent driving and maintenance.

Right: Captain F.B. Edmundson, the LRDG medical officer alongside Sheikh Abd el Galil, the leader of the Libyan Senussi resistance movement. The respected leader travelled with the LRDG during the Fezzan campaign in January 1941. He acted as a guide and to inspire the Libyans to act against the Italians.

An R Patrol truck changing a wheel while its passenger, a British agent (Flower), looks on.

A Ford F30 drives beside 'the wire'. They are carrying Arabs who may have acted as guides or were being delivered for a special operation.

Members of L Detachment SAS posing for a photograph after being rescued by Captain J.R. Easonsmith's R Patrol, November 1941. It was a disastrous paratrooper drop in a storm that led to the men being scattered and captured, killed or lost for a time. Only twenty-two men out of sixty-five dropped reached the LRDG rendezvous. Major David Stirling (tall man, centre) led the raid that was to target enemy airfields.

Major David Stirling (centre with cap) stands together with his SAS and G Patrol comrades against the 'Blitz Buggy'. This was a desert-adapted Canadian-built Ford CIIADF wood-panelled station wagon employed by the SAS. They were on the way back from the Benghazi raid in September 1942. Left: Guardsman L.A. Gibson MM, LRDG, Sergeant A.R. Seekings SAS, unidentified, Sergeant J. Cooper SAS, Stirling (behind him), 'Scotty' Scott LRDG, Trooper G. Rose SAS, Guardsman E. Murray LRDG. Standing on the vehicle is Guardsman G. Blamey LRDG. Note the SAS badge painted on the side of the vehicle.

Injured Trooper P.J. Burke is being assisted into the LRDG Waco AX697 aircraft for evacuation to hospital. His T2 Patrol comrades prepare to bid him farewell.

The Waco about to take off.

Captain P.J.D. McCraith, Y Patrol commander, in front of an F30 30cwt truck. Resting on top of the vehicle is British agent Captain Taranto, who McCraith is about to take on a 'behind-the-lines' mission.

Colonel J. Haselden, a British agent who worked among the Arabs. He was a typical 'Taxi Service' passenger, who was being carried to and from his missions far behind enemy lines. He was later killed in action leading a Commando raid on Tobruk in September 1942. The photo was taken at Siwa, next to a Westland Lysander reconnaissance aircraft. Behind him is a Ford 15cwt.

Centre: Captain J.R. Talbot with two passengers he took on a patrol. Left: Captain P. McIntyre, the official New Zealand war artist. He painted a series of LRDG watercolours and drawings. Right: Captain Chevalier, a photographer.

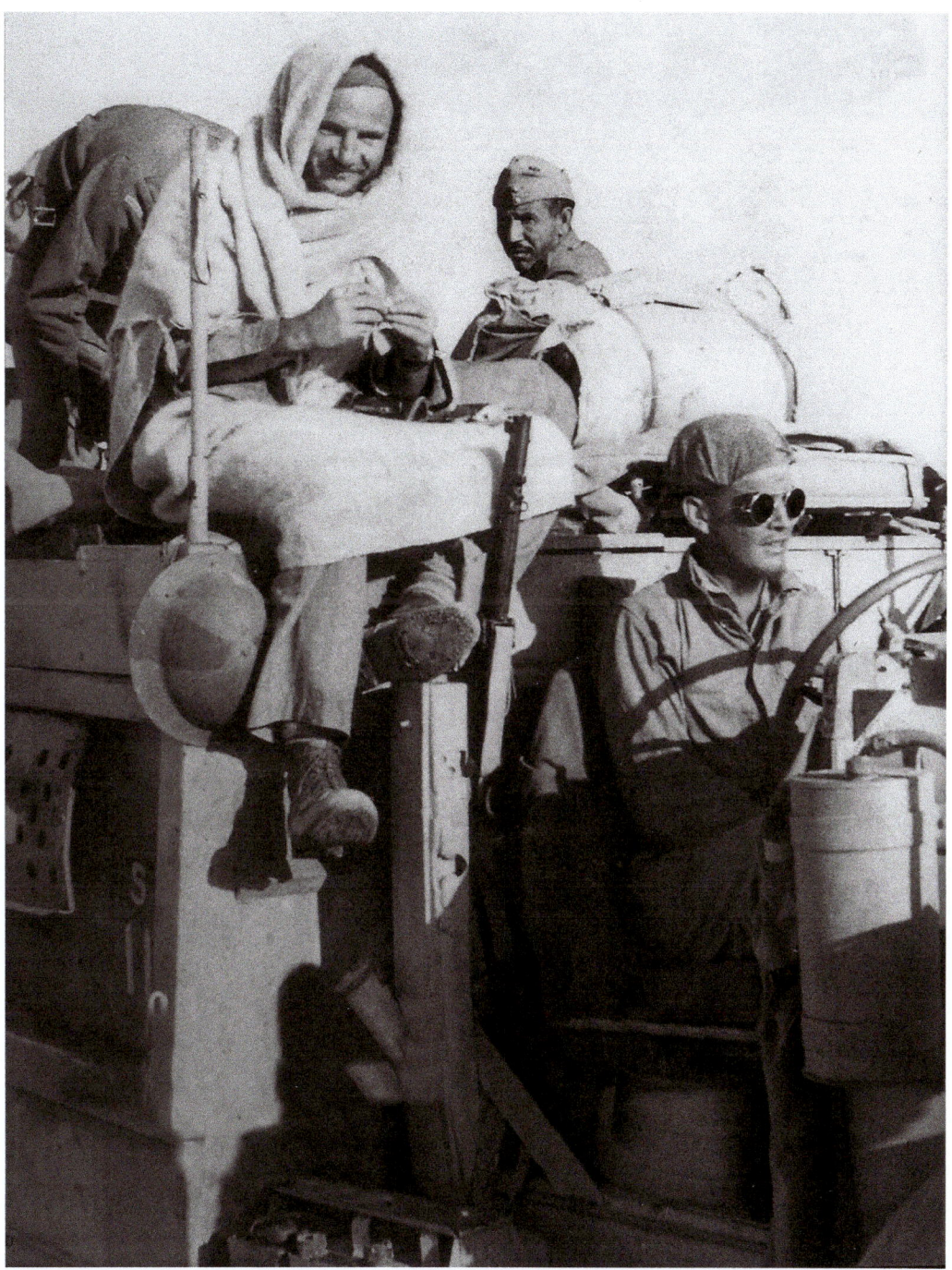
Sergeant K.T. Low of S Patrol carrying a passenger disguised as an Arab.

(**Above**) A patrol halts to talk to Arabs for intelligence-gathering or to carry them as guides.

(**Opposite, above**) R1 Patrol lined up. While on this trip they were attacked by seven Italian CR.42 fighters. An observer, Captain M. Pilkington of the Arab Legion, was killed, along with Lance Corporal N. O'Malley, patrol navigator. Private M.F. Fogden was wounded and two trucks were damaged beyond repair.

(**Opposite, below**) Following an air attack, Private M.F. Fogden was wounded in both legs. Here he rests on top of the truck transporting him to an air evacuation rendezvous. Note the unusual truck tactical sign indicating it is truck R3 of R1 Patrol. Left: Private F.J. Whitaker and Private D.O. Beale.

Private M.F. Fogden being carefully lowered into a Bristol Blenheim bomber by fellow patrol members.

A Bristol Blenheim light bomber silhouetted in the desert light at Tazerbo as it prepares to evacuate the wounded Private M.F. Fogden.

Members of Y Patrol examine an overturned RAF Westland Lysander liaison/reconnaissance aircraft, Melfa, May 1942.

Y Patrol using two trucks with cables in an attempt to right the Lysander for recovery.

A Vickers Wellington bomber crew forced to land due to engine failure. They were picked up by the LRDG. The men are unidentified, but the original photo caption describes them as follows, from left: wireless-operator, pilot, navigator and rear gunner.

RAF crew members looking pleased to have been rescued from the desert by the LRDG. The original caption did not indicate which aircraft they flew.

A De Havilland DH86 hospital plane that landed heavy at Siwa airfield, collapsing its undercarriage. Its mission was to evacuate the wounded and malaria cases to Cairo. The stranded aircraft became a target for enemy bombing raids.

Bibliography

Primary Sources

Allen, Lance Corporal Mick, LRDG Gunner/Medical Orderly. Interviewed by WO2 R.L. Kay, NZ Official Archives at HQ LRDG on 3 May 1943.
Barrett, Captain D., Quartermaster LRDG. Interviewed by WO2 R.L. Kay, NZ Official Archives at HQ LRDG on 3 May 1943.
Craw, Merlyn, LRDG T Patrol veteran, personal interviews and letters, 1998–2002
Davies, Ron, LRDG T Patrol, wartime diary extracts
Foster, Kate, *An Ordinary Man: Memoirs of Frank White* (Terrace Station, Hororata, Canterbury, New Zealand, Dryden Press, 1999)
Grimsey, Gunner C.O., R Patrol LRDG. Extracts from his diary 17 October 1940-10 February 1942.
Grimsey, Claude 'Bluey', written recollections regarding the creation of the LRP/LRDG badge, 16 June 1949.
Johnston, Bill, *LRDG Association Annual Newsletter 'Gazelles'*, 1981
Lewis, Dick, LRDG T Patrol, veteran written recollections, 1998
McGraith, Patrick, *LRDG Association Annual Newsletter 'Early Desert Operations'*, 1981
McLeod, Staff Sergeant A.F. (Archie), in charge of the LRDG Workshops. Interviewed by WO2 R.L. Kay, NZ Official Archives at HQ LRDG on 3 May 1943.
O'Carroll, Brendan, *Fighting with the Long Range Desert Group: Merlyn Craw MM's War 1940–1945* (Pen & Sword Books Ltd, Barnsley, South Yorkshire, England, 2022)
O'Carroll, Brendan, *Kiwi Scorpions: The Story of the New Zealanders in the Long Range Desert Group* (Honiton, Devon, Token Publishing, 2000)
Steele, Don, R Patrol veteran, recollection letters to Mr L.K. Kay, New Zealand War History Branch, Dept of Internal Affairs, Wellington, 12 June 1949.

The National Archives, Kew

All the following relate to Ref No. TNA: WO 201/816 268890

Report on the work of the LRDG Signals (Desert Phase), Personnel.
LRDG Operation Report No.44 by Lieutenant J.R. Talbot, R2 Patrol, 23 September 1942.
Appendix to LRDG Operation Report No.44 by Sergeant L.A. Willcox, R2 Patrol, 23 September 1942.
LRDG Operation Report No.49 by Captain L.H. Browne, 2 December 1942.
LRDG Operation Report No.50 by Sergeant J. Stocker, G2 Patrol, 23 July 1942.
LRDG Operation Report No.56 by Sergeant C. Waetford, R2 Patrol, 21 January 1943.
LRDG Operation Report No.61 by Lieutenant D. Henry, S2 Patrol, 12 November 1942.
LRDG Operation Report No.62 by Lieutenant E.F. Spicer, Y1 Patrol, 16 November 1942.
LRDG Operation Report No.65 by Second Lieutenant K.F. McLauchlan, 27 December 1942.
LRDG Operation Report No.69 by Lieutenant D. Henry, S2 Patrol, 28 November 1942.
LRDG Operation Report No.69, Appendix B, Sergeant G.H. Jackson, 27 December 1942.
LRDG Operation Report No.70 by Captain J.A.L. Timpson, G1 Patrol, 29 December 1942.
LRDG Operation Report No.81 by Captain A. Deniff, Heavy Section, 17 January 1943.
LRDG Operation Report, The Ninth Phase, October 24th 1942 to January 23rd 1942.
LRDG Situation Report Ref: CRME/12785/5/G(5): The difficulties with the Ford F30 by Lieutenant Colonel Bagnold, 1941.
General Notes of a Road Watch, 17 March to 29 March 1942 by Captain J.R. Easonsmith, R1 Patrol.

Index

Abbassia, 28, 54, 66, 117, 126, 142, 159
Abd el Galil, Sheikh, 229
Adams, L/Cpl. W.R., 51
Agheila, 185–6
Ain Dalla, 81–2, 86, 127
Ain Dua, 5, 9, 11
Ain Gazala, 224–5
Alexander, Capt. W.G., 203
Allen, L/Cpl. E.M., 159
Arger, Tpr. A., 175
Arnold, Lt. P.L., 81, 88
Atkins, Sgm. R., 201–202
Auchinleck, Gen. Sir C., 117, 142
Augila, 5, 21

Bagnold, Col. R.A., 1, 24, 40, 92, 100–101, 106, 127, 129
Bagush, 225
Bailey, Pte. A.E.F., 204
Ball, L/Cpl. C.G., 130
Ballantyne, Lt. L.B., 60, 117
Bambery, Sgt. W.R., 56
Barbour, Sgm. K.L., 118, 175
Barce, 80, 142, 146, 156, 215
Barnes, Tpr. G.M., 12
Barrett, Capt. D., 77, 82, 127
Bartliffe, Tpr. A.E., 175
Bassett, Cpl. D.M., 28
Beale, Pte. D.O., 236
Beech, Cpl. F.R., 11–12
Benghazi, 183–4, 194, 222
Big Cairn, 98
Bir el Quseir, 198
Bir es Sciueref, 210
Bir Tala, 221, 228
Blamey, Gdsm. G., 187, 231
Bond, Pte. A., 204–205
Bosdari, Vittorio, 210
Boyd, Pte. N.B., 78, 166
Brannigan, Pte. J. 204–205
Brown, Pte. A.F., 14
Brown, Pte. F.R., 12
Browne, Capt. L.H., 77, 93, 97, 225–6

Bruce, Lt. B., 187–9
Bruce, Pte. J., 50
Burgess, Tpr. W.H., 109
Burke, Tpr. P.J., 44, 232
Burnnand, Tpr. W.D., 54, 59
Butler, L/Cpl. E.G., 12

Campbell, Tpr., N.R., 97, 201
Cantley, Lt. J.E., 188
Carningham, L/Cpl. J.W., 175
Carr, L/Cpl. S.M., 175
Castel Benito, 218
Cave, Tpr. A.H., 62
Chard, Tpr. H.C., 175
Chott el Djerid, 93–5
Clayton, Maj. P.A., 1, 4–5, 50–1, 98, 163
Coombes, Tpr. L.S.A., 64
Cooper, Sgt. J., 231
Cramond, Lt. A.R., 135
Craw, Cpl. M.H., 35, 125, 156, 162
Crichton-Stuart, Capt. M.D.D., 7
Croucher, Capt. C.H.B., 10–11

Davies, L/Cpl. R.C., 44, 94, 107, 109, 144, 157, 169
Davis, Tpr. A., 175
Davis, Tpr. J.L.D., 120
Dawes, Tpr. G., 175
Denniff, Capt. A., 81–2, 118, 175
Devine, Pte. F., 185
Dimbleby, Richard, 221
Djebel Tebaga, 93
Dodunski, Tpr. A.F., 7, 12, 60, 165, 201
Dornbush, Pte. C.A., 133, 151
Du Toit, Sgm. H.P., 197–8

Easonsmith, Maj. J.R., 166, 185, 224–5, 231
Edmundson, Lt. F.B., 1, 5, 16, 24, 77, 126, 229
El Agheila, 183
Ellingham, Lt. S.W., 104, 170, 172
Emslie, Pte. J., 12
Evans, Sgm. T., 198, 203
Eyles, Tpr. J.W., 7, 12

Fayoum, 159, 200
Ferguson, Tpr. A.G., 151
Fisher, Tpr. C.L., 201
Fogden, Pte. M.F., 227–8, 236, 238–9
Fort Lamy, 44
Franks, Tpr. J.A., 191

Gabes, 93, 95
Gafsa, 96
Garven, Cpl. G.C., 7, 12, 104, 109
Giarabub, 126, 226
Gibb, Sgt. A.D., 9, 12
Gibson, Gdsm. L.A., 231
Gilf Kebir, 81
Gill, Pte. J.E., 202
Goddard, Pte. A.F., 74, 204–205
Gorringe, Tpr. R.O., 12
Graham, L/Cpl. A.C., 175
Grand Erg Oriental, 93, 109
Gravil, Dvr. J.H., 81
Grimsey, Cpl. C.O., 2, 12, 24, 31, 102, 160, 165, 203, 224–5
Gueret el Halib, 225–6
Guild, Maj. A.I., 228
Gurdon, Lt. R.B., 198–200
Gutteridge, Cpl. E., 77

Hannah, Gdsm. D., 187
Harkness, Gdsm. R., 199
Haselden, Col. J., 234
Hatiet Etla, 118
Hawkins, Pte. L.J., 15
Hayes, Tpr. R.D., 203
Hayward, Capt. T., 77
Henderson, Gnr. E.J., 205
Henry, Lt. J.D., 43, 92, 113–14, 125, 197
Hewetson, Cpl. H.P., 56
Hirst, Tpr. J.D., 175
Hofra, 187–8
Holliman, Lt. C.A., 2, 7, 85, 166, 226
Hood, Sgt. A.W., 85
Hon, 82–3, 88, 159, 175, 205, 228
Hunter, Capt. A.D., 227
Hutchins, Tpr. D.A., 61, 175

Ineson, Pte. K.C.J., 203

Jackson, Sgt. G.H., 197
Jalo, 4, 82, 142, 200, 221
Jebel Akhdar, 221–2
Jebel Sherif, 11, 51
Johnson, Bill, 126

Jopling, Tpr. F.W., 38, 122
Jordan, Sgm. B.C., 43–4, 72

Kalansho Sand Sea, 5
Kay, WO2, R.L., 81–2
Kennedy Shaw, Capt. W.B., 1, 77
Kharga Oasis, 18
Ksar Rhilane, 94–5, 107–109
Kufra, 2, 40, 42, 50, 81–2, 132, 142, 159, 167–8, 172, 184, 186, 188, 201–202, 213, 221, 226

Landon-Lane, Lt. R.J., 33, 64, 227–8
Lawson, Capt. R.P., 200
Lazarus, Lt. K.H., 188, 203
Leach, L/Cpl. F.A., 187
Lewis, Sgt. R.W.N., 40, 159
Lewis, L/Cpl. T.J., 204–205
Lloyd Owen, Capt. D., 74, 80, 166, 170
Low, Sgt. K.T., 204–205, 235

Maadi, 162
Macassey, Tpr. J.L.P., 15, 153, 177
Marada, 92, 188
Marble Arch, 183–4, 194–6
Mareth Line, 93–6
Martuba, 225
Mather, Tpr. L.F., 9, 12
Matmata, 93
McBean, Tpr. R., 109
McCallum, Pte. I.C., 80
McCorkindale, Sgt. A., 12
McCraith, Capt. P.J.D., 7, 223, 233
McCulloch, Tpr. I.G., 37, 104, 128
McDonald, Tpr. T., 169
McKeown, Tpr. F.J.W., 69
McIntyre, Capt. P., 221, 234
McIver, Pte. L.A., 28, 66
McKenzie, Pte. C.B., 109, 153–4
McLauchlan, Lt. K.F., 202
McLeod, Sgt, A.F., 42, 81, 85
McQueen, Lt. R.B., 21
Mechili, 172
Mekili, 225
Mersa Matruh, 82, 162
Miller-Kerr, L/Cpl. J., 175
Minqar Sida, 198
Misurata, 82
Mitford, Capt. E.C., 1, 5, 9, 12
Mitford, Tpr. P.V., 191
Moore, Cpl. R.J., 28, 59–60
Msus, 82

Munro, Pte. D., 109
Murray, Gdsm. E., 198–200, 231

Nelson, Gnr. G.H., 12, 165
Norton, L/Cpl. H., 203
Nutt, L/Cpl. A.H.C., 163

Ollerenshaw, Sgt. G.A., 187
O'Malley, L/Cpl. N., 227, 236

Parkes, Tpr. G.C., 12
Penfold, Sgt. Maj. J., 77
Peniakoff (Popski), Lt. Col. V., 80, 93–6, 203–204
Pilkington, Capt. M., 227, 236
Pleydell, Capt. M., 200
Prendergast, Col. G.L., 83
Pressick, L/Cpl. A., 114, 170

Ramsay, L/Cpl. R.A., 94, 109
Respinger, Bdr. A.E., 12
Rezin Pte. G.D., 114, 117
Ritchie, Tpr. T.E., 97, 122
Roderick, L/Cpl. L., 12, 51
Rommel, Gen. E., 210–11
Rose, Tpr. G., 231
Russell, Pte. E.T., 85
Ryan, Cpl. C.C., 204

Sabria, 94–5
Sadgrove, L/Cpl. A.D., 201
Saloum, 219
Sanders, Gnr. E., 152
Sandle, Pte. S.J., 175
Saunders, Tpr. A.M., 11–12, 32, 130
Saxton, Capt. C.K., 102
Schaab, L/Cpl. J.L., 85
Scott, Pte. R.N., 175
Scriven, Sgm. T., 118, 122
Searle, Sgm. D., 77
Sebha, 210
Seekings, Sgt. A.R., 231
Shepherd, Tpr. B.F., 28
Sirte, 142, 183
Siwa, 60, 62, 74, 82, 113, 131–2, 142, 159–60, 163–6, 184, 221–2, 224–5, 234, 241
Spain, Tpr. V.C., 12, 36
Special Air Service (SAS), 221, 224–5, 231
Spicer, Lt. E.F., 184, 192
Springford, Tpr. B.C., 62
Stacey, Tpr. A., 118

Steele, Maj. D.G., 1–4, 12–13, 15–16, 42, 55, 92, 113, 126, 160, 162, 221, 224
Stirling, Maj. D., 198, 224–6, 231
Stocker, Sgt. J., 198–200
Stutterd, Gnr. E.C., 15, 28
Sutherland, Lt. J.H., 5–7, 10–12

Talbot, Lt. R.J., 184, 200–202, 234
Tanner, Tpr. A., 185
Taranto, Capt., 223, 233
Tazerbo, 2, 44, 128, 159–61, 172, 226, 228, 239
Tebaga Gap, 93, 96
Tebessa, 96, 108–109
Timimi, 225
Timpson, Capt. J.A.L., 186–9, 193
Tinckler, Tpr. K., 150
Tinker, Lt. R.A., 44, 64, 93, 95–6, 120, 130, 154, 188, 205
Tippett, Tpr. K.E., 35
Tobruk, 82, 214, 234
Tozeur, 94, 96
Tripoli, 2, 94, 183–4, 194, 210, 221
Trucchi Company, 13, 185

Uweinat, 2, 4, 81

Vaughan, Gdsm. B., 200

Waco aircraft, 7, 44, 126, 133, 232
Wadi Halfa, 81–2
Wadi Hatema, 184
Wadi Tamet, 227–8
Wadi Zebaui, 188
Wadi Zem Zem, 203
Waetford, Sgt. C., 11–12, 16, 43, 161
Waetford, Pte. E.B., 161, 165
Wavell, Gen. Sir A., 1
Welsh, Gdsm. M.A., 187–8
Wheatley, Cpl. J., 186–7
Wheeldon, Sgm. H., 187–8
Whitaker, Pte. F.J., 236
White, Lt. R.F., 28, 91, 109
Whitehead, Sgm. C.H., 204
Wilder, Capt. N.P., 93, 106, 151, 215
Willcox, Tpr. L.A., 5–6, 9, 12, 200, 202
Wilson, Gdsm. A., 187, 199, 200
Wise, Tpr. H., 175

Zella, 43, 83, 159, 168–9, 188, 228
Zighen, 173, 182–2, 184
Zimmerman, Tpr. J., 85
Zouar, 160–1, 198